Chronicles from the Field

Chronicles from the Field

The Townsend Thai Project

Robert M. Townsend, Sombat Sakunthasathien, and Rob Jordan

8/29/2013

Dearest Ian and Natalya,
may you find your way
in the "field" of life, and
may your chronicles be
rich with joy.
your friends,
Rob & Shiva

The MIT Press
Cambridge, Massachusetts
London, England

MIT Press books may be purchased at special quantity discounts for business or sales promotional use. For information, please email special_sales@mitpress.mit.edu or write to Special Sales Department, The MIT Press, 55 Hayward Street, Cambridge, MA 02142.

This book was set in Palatino by Toppan Best-set Premedia Limited, Hong Kong. Printed and bound in the United States of America.

Library of Congress Cataloging-in-Publication Data

Townsend, Robert M., 1948–
Chronicles from the field : the Townsend Thai project / Robert M. Townsend, Sombat Sakunthasathien, and Rob Jordan.
   p.   cm.
Includes bibliographical references and index.
ISBN 978-0-262-01907-1 (hardcover : alk. paper)
1. Household surveys—Thailand—Methodology. 2. Households—Thailand.
3. Thailand—Social conditions—1986– 4. Thailand—Economic conditions—1986–
I. Sombat Sakunthasathien. II. Jordan, Rob, 1976– III. Title.
HN700.55.A85   2013
315.93—dc23
2012037156

10   9   8   7   6   5   4   3   2   1

Contents

Preface

Chronicles from the Field: The Townsend Thai Project tells the story of
a process, both personal and intellectual, of how the Townsend Thai
Project originated and became one of the longest-running surveys of
its kind.

Many economic and social policies are implemented without the
requisite data or appropriate frameworks for analysis. Instead, prior
convictions, political considerations, and the advice of outside experts
drive policy making. While well intended, such policies can adversely
affect those they seek to help. These criticisms are not bound to policymakers alone. Economists, as well, often fall into narrowly focused
approaches, concentrating only on micro- or macroeconomics, for
instance, rather than integrating them. This text highlights our pursuit
of collecting extensive data in the hope of better informing economic
and social policy. (Table P.1, at the end of this preface, charts the types
and extent of the surveys the project conducts, by location, number of
households, length, and other pertinent details.)

This book tells the story not only of how the Thai project originated,
but also of the challenges and rewards that come from a search to better
understand the process of development within a country. It explores
what it means to the very people who fuel that growth or perhaps get
caught up in it, for better or worse. This narrative is also a human-
interest story. The actors in the narrative are people with their own lives
and stories: the enumerators, our key field staff, and, on occasion, the
families and households themselves.

Khun Sombat Sakunthasathien, Director of Survey Operations in
Thailand, and I are grateful to our co-author, journalist Rob Jordan,
who accompanied us throughout Thailand to chronicle the work of the
Thai Family Research Project (TFRP), and who wrote the text. Sombat

spent countless hours sharing his insights with Rob Jordan and introducing him to our colleagues and the vast operation.

We hope the text will provide others with easy access to the insights we have gleaned over our 15 years of field experience. We've tried to identify the problems we encountered in doing large surveys, the lessons that we learned, and how we solved the problems we faced. While textbooks offer prescriptions and guidelines regarding best-practice standards for conducting surveys and field research, and indeed we followed these, they often fail to prepare the user for the hardest part: actual implementation.

Anyone who is interested in doing research or surveys in a developing or unfamiliar country might take particular interest in how lessons learned in Thailand can be applied to their own research endeavors. The central challenge highlighted in this book—designing, writing, and implementing a survey on such a large scale—will interest those studying survey design. Wording and translating the surveys are two additional obstacles we discuss. Readers who manage research efforts may be especially interested in our book from a human resources standpoint. Issues about pay, internal staff conflicts, hiring, endurance in the face of setbacks and fatigue, and other challenges surface throughout the book in often unexpected ways. Finally, given Thailand's beauty, diversity, and its growing place in the world economy, historians, students, and scholars will appreciate this window into Thai culture, both its modernity and its quiet, often-overlooked populations.

It is our hope that this book will supplement the learning experience of researchers worldwide and provide them with a practical text for their efforts.

Of special note: A compelling documentary film titled *Emerging Thailand: The Spirit of Small Enterprise* directly complements this book. For more information on the film, go to http://www.emergingthailand.org.

Acknowledgments

I would like to highlight my good friend and the central figure in the book: Mr. Sombat Sakunthasathien, or "Khun Sombat" as he is known to his peers. Khun Sombat's skepticism about top-down policies made us fast friends. I found in Khun Sombat a rare combination of the ability to work in the field with villagers and the finesse needed to navigate Bangkok offices. Khun Sombat is the main character in the drama that has evolved on the ground since the mid-1990s when we met. The onetime government bank official, gas station entrepreneur, and travel guide has steered TFRP through deaths and births and government power struggles. A pioneer, Khun Sombat has taken TFRP to the most remote corners of Thailand, defending it against armed, cross-border bandits and thieving frog hunters. He has served as a politician, CEO, and friend to government officials, enumerators, and household interviewees. His belief that one can determine what is going on by patient, caring, and gentle probing has proven critical time and time again. I'll let the narrative in the chapters speak for itself, but let me reiterate that meeting Khun Sombat changed my life. It gave rise to a close personal friendship and an economic survey operation that has realized our vision.

I would also like to thank the TFRP staff. Without the efforts of those in the field in Thailand, the survey would not be implemented and available for use to researchers around the world: Panida Tanapoltaveerat, supervisor; Tiptanradee Panchayayodanan, supervisor; Pavisanat Pathomchareonsukchai, supervisor; Tippatavee Pathomcharoensukchai, supervisor; Laddawan Kamkoa, supervisor; Thanatyakorn Sangkornthiraphut, supervisor; Thanatyakorn Sangkornthiraphut, supervisor, soil and water work; Panadda Thongsiri, field editor (Lop Buri); Wattanachai Jangsawang, field editor (Sisaket); Pilawan Kamkoa, field editor (Buriram); Kanlaya Lerkdee, field editor (Chachoengsao); and all of our survey enumerators over the years.

I owe a special thanks to other researchers whose efforts in our early days have made the survey a success. Anna Paulson was a co-principal investigator on the first grant that funded the first large survey in 1997. Anna and Tae Jeong Lee were very much part of the design of survey instruments and pretests. Michael Binford helped select survey areas within provinces.

Staff members at the University of Chicago were particularly helpful in getting this manuscript to this stage. I would like to thank Christina Gebel, Natalie Hoover El Rashidy, Jennifer Ptak, Jennifer Roche, and the research assistants who provided valuable feedback and editing, including Kevin Jones, Brittany Piovesan, Stefanie Stantcheva, and Martin Wolberg-Stock. Leslie Athey helped us highlight important lessons for survey design and data collection. I thank Kathleen Parks and the National Opinion Research Center (NORC) at the University of Chicago for continuing collaboration on grants and surveys. The Department of Economics and Social Sciences Division at the University of Chicago has also been essential to my work. I remain a research associate there, and I run the Consortium on Financial Systems and Poverty. I continue to work and collaborate with faculty and students at Chicago from my home as Elizabeth & James Killian Professor of Economics at the Massachusetts Institute of Technology (MIT). In turn, MIT has entered into a collaborative agreement with the University of the Thai Chamber of Commerce (UTCC), and many MIT faculty and students are engaged in the Thai project. MIT and Chicago staff, faculty, and students all work together, and we find our family of researchers is ever growing. Indeed, without the effort of many staff and colleagues worldwide, this project would have never been as extensive or noteworthy as it has become. I would like to express my sincere thanks to all who have been a large or small part of this story.

Robert M. Townsend

Box P.1

Common Abbreviations Used	
BAAC	Bank for Agriculture and Agricultural Cooperatives
CDD	Ministry of the Interior's Community Development Department
ICRISAT	International Crops Research Institute for the Semi-Arid Tropics
NESDB	National Economic and Social Development Board
NSO	Thai National Statistics Office
SES	Socioeconomic Survey
UTCC	University of the Thai Chamber of Commerce

Common Thai Language Words Used	
Amphoe	District
Changwat	Province
Khun	A form of address, meant to communicate respect, like "Mr." or "Mrs." Thai names are characterized by a first or given name, followed by a family name. Family names can be long and complicated and, unlike other countries, are changed relatively frequently. Thai address each other by a given name, preceded by either Khun or a title of public distinction, for government officials. Most Thai have informal nicknames (seldom relating to the given name); in everyday life, a Thai is introduced by nickname, not by given name.
Tambon	An area of size falling between a district and a village

Table P.1
Overview of the Townsend Thai Data Surveys

Name of Survey	Baseline Survey	Rural Annual Resurvey	Monthly Resurvey	Urban Annual Resurvey
Year Initiated	May 1997	1998 to present	1999 to present	2005 to present
Description	Initial cross-sectional survey spanning four provinces	Longitudinal, or panel, data collected annually from 1/3 of households in the Baseline Survey	Intensive, micro-level cross-sectional survey collected monthly from a subset of villages in the Baseline Survey	Panel data collected annually in urban areas within provinces in the Rural Annual Resurvey
Provinces	Chachoengsao, Lop Buri, Buriram, and Sisaket	Chachoengsao, Lop Buri, Buriram, Sisaket, Phrae, and Satun (Yala and Phetchabun—2003, 2004 only)	Chachoengsao, Lop Buri, Buriram, and Sisaket	Chachoengsao, Lop Buri, Buriram, Sisaket, Phrae, and Satun
Number of Households[1]	2,880	1,228	682	1,440
Attrition	N/A	2.5%	1.3%	2.6%
Survey Instruments	Household Key Informant Financial Institution BAAC Environmental Aerial Photos	Household Key Informant Financial Institution BAAC (2000) Environmental	Household Environmental	Household Key Informant Financial Institution Environmental
Amount of Time for Each Instrument	Household: 1.66 hours Key Informant: 1 hour Financial Institution: 1.25 hours BAAC: 1.25 hours	Household: 1.66 hours Key Informant: 1 hour Financial Institution: 1.25 hours BAAC: 1.25 hours	Monthly: 4–6 hours, made up of three to four 1–1.5 hour long interviews completed within 30–40 days of each interview round	Household: 1.66 hours Key Informant: 1 hour Financial Institution: 1.25 hours

1. Numbers indicated as of October 2011.

Introduction: The History of the Townsend Thai Surveys

Running since 1997 and continuing still today, the Townsend Thai Data is arguably one of the most remarkable, unique, and extensive datasets in the world. It represents more than 15 years of annual data for 985 households and monthly data on 680 households running for more than 150 continuous months.[1] It has tracked millions of observations about the financial and entrepreneurial activities of households and institutions in rural and urban settings for this rising developing country. Furthermore, the dataset is remarkable for its integrity: nearly 97 percent of households return to participate in the survey from year to year.

Today the project helps bridge the divide between policy and research by providing rich data from which academics and policymakers can better understand household financial activities and behavior and how household decisions have an impact on the regional and national economy. Such detailed data, taken from the same households and institutions over time (i.e., *panel data*), allow researchers to test economic models in ways that have not been possible before. While the most direct benefit of this work has been for Thailand, economic models developed there have been applied to other developing countries, such as Mexico. Knowledge gained from the research is relevant for policymakers around the world, who can then make more informed decisions in their respective countries.

The Townsend Thai Project

Early in 1997, with Khun Sombat Sakunthasathien as head of survey operations in Thailand, Robert M. Townsend and collaborators set up the Thai Family Research Project (TFRP) to operate with the support of grant funding from the US government. This effort has now become an operation of over 70 employees with a central office in Nakorn Patom and four field outposts in Chachoengsao, Lop Buri, Sisaket, and Buriram. The resulting data from the surveys are termed the Townsend Thai Data.[2]

In 2004, the University of Chicago joined with the University of the Thai Chamber of Commerce (UTCC) to create the University of Chicago–UTCC Research Center in Bangkok, with the primary responsibility of collaborating with government offices in Thailand to bring together and document existing secondary data. The term "Thai Project" is used throughout this book to refer to this loosely structured data collection of institutions and partnerships in Thailand, including TFRP, Townsend Thai Data, and the UC–UTCC Research Center.

The University of Chicago–UTCC Research Center has been instrumental in archiving data complementary to the Townsend Thai Data. These data include microeconomic data on households and firms, as well as macroeconomic data from the Bank of Thailand and the National Economic and Social Development Board (NESDB). Village-level data from Thailand's Community Development Department (CDD) and provincial-level domestic product data from the NESDB add to the knowledge on Thailand's economy. At a broader level, the National Statistics Office (NSO) collects data on not only the economy, but also population, the environment and energy, industry and construction, information and communications, as well as agriculture and fisheries. This information is equally valuable to researchers.

The Townsend Thai Data

TFRP enumerators, those who implement the survey and record the responses, canvass households, financial institutions, and community leaders from Thailand's mountainous north to its sandy far south. Every year they complete thousands of highly detailed survey interviews, traversing miles of highways, dirt roads, and rice paddy paths on their rounds. They parse everything from moisture in the soil to hypothetical financial crises. How do people get by? What helps? What hurts?

The Townsend Thai Data consist of several survey instruments, with the initial baseline survey conducted in 1997 and resurveys continuing to present day. Annual resurveys capture information from households, financial institutions, BAAC groups, and village leaders. More intensive, monthly resurveys collect even more detailed data on households.

The actual survey questions have been crafted and honed through tens of thousands of interviews over more than a decade. The survey data—highly thorough and, at times, unusually intimate—are then put through rigorous analysis. A farmer's casual comments about his soybean yield or a shop owner's tale of bankruptcy go through multiple layers of cross-checking and vetting before being turned out as "clean" data, available to researchers around the globe. It's not enough to ask questions. A data and analysis system must ensure reliable answers.

Choosing Thailand and Seeking Answers

Something about Thailand intrigued Townsend during his first trip there in the early 1980s. He had traveled through Asia and was stunned by the contrasts. Hyper-modern Japan was a world apart from Hong Kong's street market atmosphere and Singapore's modern shopping malls. Thailand was altogether different: a society driven both by bartering and ingenuity, where entrepreneurial merchants ferried huge loads on their two-stroke motorbikes.

The diverse and vibrant economies of Thailand, Japan, Singapore, and Hong Kong warranted examination and raised myriad questions. (See a map of the region in figure 0.1.) What did these Asian juggernauts share? Why had they grown so rapidly? What paths had they taken toward economic success? How did the growth of national industry and markets affect local village life?

Townsend began his career studying fragmented landholdings in medieval English villages (Townsend 1993).[3] He found that individuals in these villages diversified their land holdings in order to deal with risks like floods and insects. This insight led him to India where he analyzed consumption and income patterns in a panel data set gathered

Box 0.1
Thailand and Other Asian Countries

With a population of 67 million and a land area of 514,000 square kilometers, Thailand is roughly the size of Spain. Other than its southern neighbor Malaysia, Thailand's GDP of 318 billion USD is higher than other surrounding countries. Thailand's primary export commodities comprise textiles, footwear, fishery products, rice, rubber, jewelry, automobiles, computers, and electrical appliances.

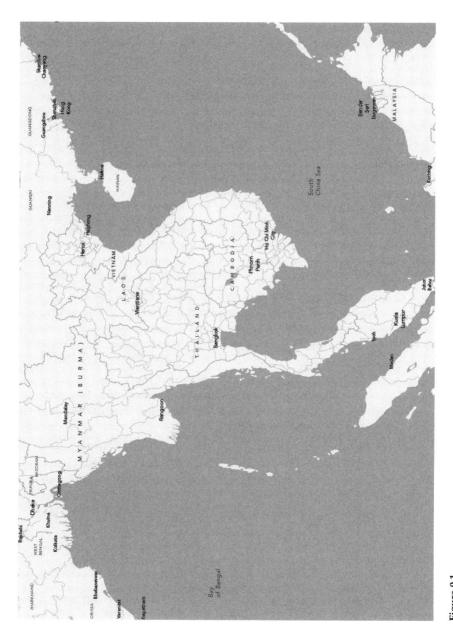

Figure 0.1
Map of Southeast Asia

by the International Crops Research Institute for the Semi-Arid Tropics, or ICRISAT (Townsend 1994).[4] Townsend, again, looked at the strategies that households used to mitigate risks. Surprisingly, the households in village India came close to the standards suggested by economic theory: Households were taking on a proportion of the risks that affected everyone and pooling the ones they could avoid.

These findings were surprising to some in policy and academic circles. How could informal, indigenous institutions function so well? Perhaps transfers, or government payments to households, needed to be focused on villages and not individual households within villages?

Townsend wanted to see if households had ways to deal optimally with these risks they face. Also, he wanted to examine if the challenges households experienced affected all households or only some and not others. Finding answers to these questions would allow him to evaluate what was happening in an actual economy, compared to what models said should happen if things are efficient.

While Townsend's previous work provided an initial understanding about how villages manage risk, he was limited by the data available. Thailand offered him a village setting and the opportunity to overcome those previous limitations. His visits to northeast Thailand and more sustained field research in the north revealed that informal financial systems, such as gift giving and informal credit, seemed to vary across villages, even between those near to one another in arguably similar environments. Likewise, the role of outside, more formal financial institutions, like banks, varied as well. What was the source of this informal village-level variation? How well could the formal financial sector, or national level institutions like banks, address these issues if their reach was uneven? These questions, the opportunity to collect data, and the desire to better understand how economies were put together from the ground up convinced Townsend that Thailand was a ripe environment in which to begin to understand the elements of economic growth and development.

History of the Baseline Survey

With these questions in mind, Townsend and Khun Sombat went to the field with TFRP enumerators in April 1997 to conduct the first baseline survey. They decided to collect and construct a snapshot of the socio-economic conditions of rural villagers: who made up the household, what they did for a living, what kinds of economic activities they engaged in, and what kind of financial services they used and how often, among others.

While the process was instructive on its own, Townsend knew he would need more information than a traditional household survey could provide. In addition, he needed to include survey instruments to study villages, local financial institutions, and also lending groups. Households, villages, and *tambons* (an area the size of a county) were selected at random from two separate regions: the more highly developed central region, located near Bangkok, and the poorer, semi-arid northeast.

All told, enumerators gathered information on 2,880 households, 192 key informants (or village headmen), 161 financial institutions, and 262 BAAC groups as part of the initial baseline survey. It also included the collection of soil samples and photos from 1,920 individual farm plots with an accompanying soil questionnaire.

Expanding the Survey

The baseline survey was designed as a one-time survey. However, with the onset of the Asian financial crisis of July 1997, the Ford Foundation funded what turned out to be the first annual resurvey in the spring of 1998, in 64 villages, to gauge the impact of the crisis.

Since then, the annual survey has expanded. In 2003, the southern provinces of Satun and Yala were added, and a year later the northern provinces of Phrae and Phetchabun were added. Data collection in Satun and Phrae continues to date. In 2005, with the help of the Thai Ministry of Finance, the annual survey was expanded to include 480 urban households across the survey's provinces. Currently, the annual survey consists of 15 years of continuous annual data for 985 households in both urban and rural areas.

While the annual survey provides broader cross-sectional information, a monthly survey was implemented in 1998, which provides detailed data that are more easily collected through frequent interviews. The monthly survey interviews a subset of households in the 1997 baseline survey from 16 total villages across 4 provinces: Chachoengsao, Lop Buri, Buriram, and Sisaket. The primary goal was a microlevel evaluation of family networks, markets, and formal institutions in credit and insurance. Currently, the monthly resurvey spans over 14 years and reaches approximately 720 households.

In addition to these data, TFRP has collected detailed environmental data. It was important for Townsend to include environmental data in his research because such data could allow researchers to understand how a household's surroundings might influence the shocks they experience, such as flooding and drought, and how they react to and recover from those shocks.

Together, these data provide a very detailed picture of daily life for thousands of Thai households. Over the years, the surveys have not been conducted in a vacuum. Various historical and government milestones (see figure 0.2) have intermingled with the timing of the surveys.

Funding

Both the annual and monthly surveys have relied on multiple sources of funding for their completion. As with any successful survey, funding is essential. It is only because of the funding secured and the support and vision of the project's funders that the Townsend Thai Data can sustain such longevity.

The Thai surveys have primarily been funded by US federal agencies, the bulk of it by the National Institute of Child Health and Human Development (NICHD)[5] in a series of five-year grants. The University of the Thai Chamber of Commerce (UTCC) has generously supported the monthly surveys. Other contributing organizations include the National Science Foundation,[6] which funded part of the Thai infrastructure and a relatively more substantial part of research back in Chicago. The Thai Ministry of Finance supported the first urban survey in 2005, and UTCC supports its continuation. The BAAC helped finance initial survey operations in the south with its physical and human infrastructure. The Ford Foundation funded the resurvey in 1998, and the Andrew W. Mellon Foundation and the University of Chicago supported the initial environmental data. There have been smaller supplemental grants over time—from the University of Chicago for the environmental research and from the National Opinion Research Center (NORC). A grant from the John Templeton Foundation allowed Townsend to conduct further research using the data and look more closely at the role that enterprise plays in wealth creation and poverty alleviation. The Consortium on Financial Systems and Poverty (CFSP), through a grant from the Bill & Melinda Gates Foundation, supports some of Townsend's research on the design of the financial systems and their impact on the poor.

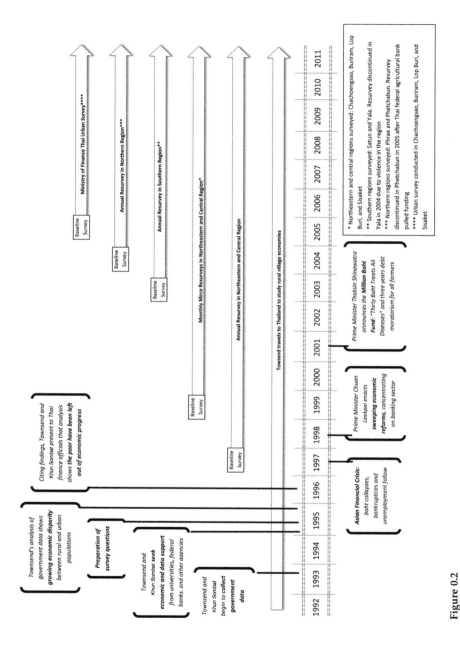

Figure 0.2
Townsend Thai Data Timeline

The Story

With this support, the Thai project moves forward. Its role in the global debate on development will likely only grow, as high-profile development campaigns realize the necessity to rely on hard, thorough data to inform decision making.

Various questions are vital to citizens and national leaders alike as they focus on how to weather environmental disasters, terrorism, and other cross-border problems that can be exacerbated by economic stagnation. Calls to increase foreign aid and forgive poor nations' debt grow, while concern mounts over the efficacy of certain aid programs and the stability of some financial lenders.

The story of how the Thai Project went from an idea shared by Robert M. Townsend and Khun Sombat Sakunthasathien to a highly organized, multimillion-dollar undertaking is about facts and figures as well as people, their aspirations, struggles, and lessons learned. Khun Sombat's story, his partnership with Townsend, and the story of those who work with him—a true extended family—is the foundation and framework of TFRP. Their story is the narrative thread behind this intensive look at one of the developing world's greatest economic success stories and the effort to document it thoroughly.

With much of the public awareness of poverty driven by political platitudes and emotionally manipulative images, the Townsend Thai Project offers a sober alternative: accurate measurement based on thoroughly collected data. Through this approach, a clear template emerges for understanding poverty and identifying paths to alleviating it.

1   Discovering a Country and a Collaborator

It was 1993, and Khun Sombat Sakunthasathien had been living in the mountain ranges of northern Thailand for almost ten months. He was far from home and missed his daughters, now nine and seven years old. He was headed to the nearest city, Chiang Mai, five hours away. A soft hotel bed, a hot shower, and a beer awaited his arrival.

As deputy director of the research department at Thailand's federal Bank for Agriculture and Agricultural Cooperatives (BAAC), Khun Sombat had been conducting a study on how to create a credit program for the area's impoverished hill tribes. Most of these refugees from Laos, Myanmar (formerly Burma), China, and northern Vietnam lacked legal status, land ownership, or collateral of any kind. The study was part of a larger German-led project, in cooperation with Thai government agencies, to help hill tribes outside Chiang Mai and in the eastern Golden Triangle area move away from poppy cultivation. The blooms that cover great swaths of this region's mountainsides every January drive an opium trade that is among the largest in the world. Their cultivation through slash-and-burn farming by Hmong, Lizu, Akha, Wa, and Taiyai people leaves steep slopes bare and susceptible to massive erosion. Access to improved healthcare, clean water, and credit would, it was hoped, lessen the poppy's allure. Khun Sombat's goal was unprecedented and fraught with political controversy.

Piloting an off-road motorcycle, Khun Sombat would go from village to village, each little more than a collection of wood huts on stilts, dodging water buffalo and roaming pigs. Over rice and vegetables in the evening, Khun Sombat introduced the concept of community savings groups to the villagers. It was a way to create collateral for loans, he told them, and a way to plan for their children's future. He handed out bank passbooks to grade school teachers and helped set up small-scale student savings groups.

Box 1.1
Bank for Agriculture and Agricultural Cooperatives (BAAC)

> The Bank for Agriculture and Agricultural Cooperatives (BAAC) in Thailand is a state enterprise whose goal is to aid farmers and rural communities to increase agricultural yields through favorable financial terms. By offering financial services, like a more traditional bank, BAAC has filled a void in rural areas where such banks otherwise do not exist. With the inauguration of the Million Baht Village Fund (see chapter 6, box 6.2), BAAC also became the fulcrum through which funds were distributed to the nearly 78,500 communities to benefit from the program.

Khun Sombat arranged for monthly collections of loan repayments and later, with a special governmental decree that allowed him to lend to non-Thai, established small BAAC offices in some mountain villages. In the mixed-tribe village of Doi Wawi in the Golden Triangle, the local savings groups—each with fewer than 40 households—have since managed to amass more than 300 million baht (about 9 million USD)[1] and secure an equivalent amount in credit. This helped make the BAAC's local lending office the most productive branch in the region. Once a month, Khun Sombat came down from the mountains to update his colleagues at the BAAC office in Chiang Mai.

Not long after he had checked into the Vista Hotel, a simple two-story concrete structure in downtown Chiang Mai, Khun Sombat received an odd note: "Mr. Townsend," it stated, "will meet you in the lobby at 6:00 this evening."

Khun Sombat was puzzled. Townsend? Who is he? It had been a long few weeks, and Khun Sombat was in little mood to entertain strangers. He wanted to be alone for a while, relax, maybe meet a friend or two later.

When Townsend arrived, he explained that he was an economics professor, staying in Chiang Mai with his wife's family between long stints in the hills. During these forays to the region's remote corners, he took notes on the village economies he encountered. He too was interested in rural economies, having studied risk and insurance in Indian villages. He had heard about Khun Sombat at BAAC's main Bangkok office. When he was told that Pee Bat, or "older brother" Khun Sombat, was working in the Chiang Mai area, Townsend went to the branch office there. He had waited three days for Khun Sombat to return.

As an economist, Townsend could not resist seeking answers. So, he had borrowed his mother-in-law's van and set out to do field research, equipped with little more than his wallet and an adequate command of the Thai language. Sleeping in one-room schools and the homes of village headmen, Townsend made his way across Thailand's remote north for weeks at a time.

A small grant from the Rockefeller Foundation paid for assistants and translators. Envisioning a larger scope and scale to the effort, Townsend was looking for partners. Meetings with various government agencies proved less than fruitful; most ministries had predetermined programs and few were receptive to the idea that data and research could help policy. It was also hard to share his vision without concrete specific accomplishments in hand.

Townsend realized he needed to adjust his focus. His first priority would be to find someone with the experience and shared vision to carry out the project, someone who could ensure quality data. It had to be someone who understood the research mission, embraced the hard work involved, had a strong sense of intellectual curiosity, and appreciated the potential payoff for Thailand. Townsend would need to create an innovative organization. Economic theory would be the survey's foundation, the source of its questions.

In the lobby of the Vista Hotel, Khun Sombat was impressed by Townsend's knowledge and polite persistence. He agreed to meet with the professor the next evening, and apologized for the inconvenience. *"Mai pen lai krap"* ("Please, it's no problem"), Townsend said before leaving.

The next night, Khun Sombat and Townsend shared a *tuk-tuk* (a motorized rickshaw) from the Vista Hotel to the bustling night market. Over freshwater mussels, rice, and Singha beer at a food stall, they discussed Khun Sombat's work in the mountains with hill tribes and Townsend's study of financial risk and insurance in Indian and medieval English villages.

Thailand might have the same—perhaps greater—potential as a case study, Townsend told Khun Sombat. He did not mention any specific plans, and Khun Sombat did not think to ask. The two agreed to continue the conversation a few days later when Khun Sombat would return to his Bangkok office.

Back in Bangkok, Townsend and Khun Sombat paid a fateful visit to the National Statistics Office (NSO). The NSO's general director reacted with bemused surprise to Townsend's request. The professor wanted public data from a federal household survey taken every five years from 1957 to 1987 and every two years thereafter. No one had ever asked for early years of the data from the Thai Household Socio-economic Study (SES), the general director said. To transfer the reams of information within Townsend's timeline would require overtime staff pay. When Townsend realized he was short the 4,000 baht (about 120 USD) needed to cover the overtime cost, Khun Sombat dug into his wallet for 1,000 baht.

Increasingly intrigued by Townsend's focus and the information he was uncovering, Khun Sombat helped the professor secure secondary financial data at various other federal and local offices. They scored another valuable haul at the Ministry of the Interior's Community Development Department (CDD). Khun Sombat approached the CDD's director, someone whose work he respected tremendously, and asked for help. The director, Yuwat Wuthimethi, responded enthusiastically. He gave Khun Sombat about five years' worth of statistical data track-ing village-level access and use of federal development resources.

Combined, the SES and CDD data represented extremely valuable information. They were the country's only available statistics collected continually and suited for economic research. No one had used them in combination before, and no one had used them to look at macro-level economic and social issues.

With two months until his next BAAC posting, Khun Sombat went a step further and arranged for Townsend to take a three-week tour of various locales featured in the SES study. Together, they crossed Thai-land's middle swath, visiting the cities of Petchaburi, Chachoengsao, Sisaket, and Nakon Ratchasima. They interviewed dozens of farmers, shopkeepers, and bankers. The wide-ranging conversations tended to center around cultivation techniques, savings practices, and education issues.

After the tour, Townsend thanked Khun Sombat profusely and boarded a plane back to Chicago. The professor cradled, like a child, his carry-on baggage stuffed with statistical documents the two men had collected. It was the last Khun Sombat would see or hear from Townsend for almost a year and a half.

Townsend's visit had planted a seed with Khun Sombat. By 1994, he had been with the BAAC for 20 years and wanted to shift gears to more theoretical work. He was also frustrated that his advice to help estab-lish rural savings and credit collectives had gone unheeded at the bank. The bank simply wanted clients for loans. Khun Sombat wanted to establish dependable, local financial organizations. So he left and went to work for a federal production credit association, where he directed a study of how to consolidate group savings.

During this time, Khun Sombat helped form a joint venture between the federal production credit association and smaller associations around Thailand, called Channabot Kao Na, or Rural Progress. As manager of the company, Khun Sombat steered funds into the purchase of seven Maxima-brand gas stations around the country. The investment appeared wise at first, and money poured in. But one year later, Thailand entered a short-term oil crisis, and disagreements among the joint venture's various members pushed Khun Sombat to sell off his interests.

For the first time that he could remember, Khun Sombat had no solid footing. He was confused about where to turn next. He had more free time on his hands than ever before.

While sorting through paperwork to dissolve the gas station business, Khun Sombat found something that seemed like a prophecy at the time. It was Townsend's address, scrawled across a creased sheet of note paper. Wondering what had become of Townsend, Khun Sombat wrote to Chicago.

A response came quickly. Townsend would be returning to Thailand with his wife in a few months. He had analyzed the SES data and had noticed something interesting. Could Khun Sombat spare some time?

In Chicago, Townsend had not been idle. He had been tinkering with design ideas for a large-scale survey, picking regions and villages using the SES data. The scope and scale Townsend envisioned would require a lot of money. He had begun applying for funding from various sources, especially US federal agencies. Funding was slow in coming.

In August 1995, Townsend reconnected with Khun Sombat in Bangkok. The two pored over Townsend's findings. Major indicators—income, accessibility to financial institutions, and education, for example—showed a profound disparity between Thailand's rural and urban populations. Development funds were not reaching many who needed them.

None of this was unusual for an average developing country. In fact, a short trip into urban or rural areas revealed the disparity to the naked eye. However, Thailand's booming economy was far from average—with annual gross domestic product growth averaging 6.2 percent for almost five decades and peaking at twice that in the 1980s (see figure 1.1). How had it grown so rapidly with such profound weaknesses?

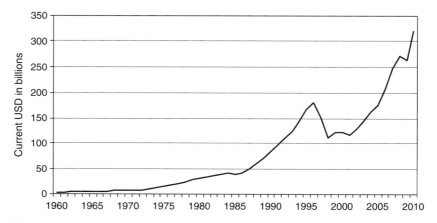

Figure 1.1
Thai GDP 1960–2010 *Source:* World Bank

How could its growth be sustained? What did the future hold—both for Thailand and other developing countries that had latched on to Thailand's economic model?

No single economic theory could explain the situation, but, Townsend argued, a study that linked theories at macro- and micro-levels might reveal the true story. It wasn't clear what factors had ignited Thailand's economy, and few attempts had been made to conduct a thorough analysis of how average Thais made do in this new economy of super-latives. The time was right to address these questions.

Khun Sombat was intrigued. He was struck by the fact that an accomplished economist from the University of Chicago considered Thailand's rural economy to be an ideal case study. Surely there was something to it.

Looking for help in collecting further data and setting up a survey, Khun Sombat and Townsend visited institutions such as the BAAC, the Bank of Thailand, Thammasat University (one of the country's presti-gious bastions of higher education), and the NESDB. At each stop, officials offered tea and listened politely. Very interesting, some said. But, what was the point of a complex, expensive study?

Thus, it was left up to the professor and the banker.

Townsend was confident he could find funding to get a survey off the ground, but he needed help. He needed a partner in Thailand, someone who would be devoted to the project. He needed someone to oversee aspects of the project ranging from staff and budget management to persuasion of and coordination with local leaders. He needed both an executive and a diplomat. He turned to Khun Sombat.

Excited by the prospect of combining his expertise, curiosity, and desire to contribute to his country, Khun Sombat said yes on the spot. There was no discussion of pay.

The son of a top official in the national revenue department, Khun Sombat was literally born into economics. As the second of six children in his family, he looked up to an older family friend for career advice. Economics, the friend told him, was like a human heart within the body of society. Once you understand the heart's rhythms, you understand the whole system. The line would echo in Khun Sombat's head years later when he recognized it as the heart of Townsend's applied general equilibrium analysis (AGE). AGE is the study not only of supply and demand but also of all market factors such as labor, capital, land, goods, and services, the reasons behind individual decisions, and, by extension, the functioning of villages, towns, regions, and nations.

As a fresh-faced 21-year-old, Khun Sombat went from Thammasat University to the BAAC where he would quickly make a name for himself as somewhat of a maverick. He had wanted to work for the bank's branch in the far northern Chang Rai region, to him, a mystical province that promised adventure and attractive girls. But the bank president placed Khun Sombat in his hometown, Nakon Chaisi, outside Bangkok. While disappointed initially, Khun Sombat saw opportunity.

At the time, heavy flooding in the Nakon Chaisi area had wiped out cropland and led to high default rates among farmers. Khun Sombat persuaded bank officials to give him authorization for numerous new loans. The money would go toward rebuilding and would be repaid in installments as farmers could regain financial stability. While waiting for the repayments, Khun Sombat regularly left his desk to visit clients and check on their progress. He helped them explore options for flood insurance—something many had never heard of before—and invited them to drop in on him anytime to discuss concerns, ask questions, or just chat.

Khun Sombat was no regular banker. For his 23rd birthday, dozens of his clients held a surprise party that kicked off with celebratory shotgun fire.

While working with BAAC, Khun Sombat won a Japanese government scholarship to attend a master's degree program in agricultural finance at Kyushu University. BAAC officials approved the three-year program on the condition that Khun Sombat would return to the bank afterward.

Living on a stipend, Khun Sombat managed to return home only twice during his studies in Japan—financing his airfare by selling Japanese watches to friends.

When Khun Sombat returned to Thailand for good, he started a family and quickly climbed the ranks of the BAAC in Bangkok, becoming a deputy director at age 30. His unique hands-on approach to banking and his role as head of BAAC's research department took him on countless adventures, from night fishing with a polygamous village headman in the far south to explaining the uses of refrigeration to a hill tribesman in the far north.

Khun Sombat was a pioneering risk taker equally at home in a polished Bangkok office or a remote tribal village without plumbing and electricity. He learned about planting techniques from poor rice farmers and lectured on rural finance to national leaders in Nepal, Indonesia, the Philippines, Malaysia, and Germany, among other places. But his greatest challenge was yet to come.

When Khun Sombat signed on to lead what came to be called the Thai Family Research Project and the Townsend Thai surveys, he had only an inkling of the scope it would soon take on. He assumed the project would last one year, for one survey. Afterward, he might work as a guide for Japanese tourists—something he had done briefly years earlier—arranging vacations at a friend's small resort on Samet Island in the South China Sea.

Townsend envisioned a survey of households, community leaders, and informal and formal financial institutions, such as the BAAC and local rice banks. Soil and water testing would be a component, providing information on environmental shocks, such as drought and flooding (see table 1.1). To ensure comparative baseline data, four provinces (*changwats*) were chosen in total: two in the central region—Lop Buri and Chachoengsao—and two in the northeast—Sisaket and Buriram. These particular provinces were chosen because each contained one district (*amphoe*) that had been sampled every year of the Thai Household Socioeconomic Survey (SES), thus providing benchmark information. Within each of the 4 provinces, 12 *tambons* (counties) were selected at random. Within each *tambon*, 4 villages were selected at random.

The survey would seek to answer one central question: What role do informal institutions, such as the family, play in helping to support the welfare and well-being of individuals in semi-urban and rural areas

Table 1.1:
Types of Survey Instruments

Survey Instrument	Information Recorded
Household	The household instrument solicits data on household composition, income, consumption, risk response, assets (including those for agriculture), borrowing, lending, saving, and business activity. The household head or spouse are interviewed and answer questions that pertain to the entire household.
Key Informant	The key informant instrument solicits data on the characteristics of the village headman (occupation, schooling, age, etc.) and, most widely, characteristics of the village, including migration, unemployment and occupation, social networks, credit and savings organizations, prices, heath, natural disasters, and risk response.
Institutional	The institutional instrument solicits data on the characteristics of respondents and their respective organization, including activities such as savings, lending, nonfinancial services, the formation of the institution and its current structure, characteristics of members and clients, internal savings and lending activities, extended repayment of loans and default, income-generating activities, current relationships with other financial institutions outside the village, and free aid.
BAAC	The BAAC instrument solicits data concerning the operations of the Bank of Agriculture and Agricultural Cooperatives (BAAC). The BAAC is similar to other banks in that it offers financial services to farmers in rural areas, which are recorded and included in the Townsend Thai Data.
Environmental	The environmental data are collected using rain gauges, soil moisture / stress meters, soil thermometers, and photography, both aerial and ground. Some of these measurements are taken on a daily or weekly basis.

of Thailand? It would focus on financial risk and the role of personal networks in an economy experiencing growth, fluctuation, and perhaps crisis. By the fall of 1995, however, the project remained little more than an idea.

In November of that year, Khun Sombat, Townsend, and two other academics Townsend recruited—Michael Binford, a University of Florida geologist and zoologist, and Alan Kolata, an anthropologist from the University of Chicago—ventured out into the field. The group traveled for almost a month in the poor northeast region of Isan. At each stop, Binford, a jovial Texan with a taste for super-spicy food, examined soil and water. The tall, loquacious Kolata, the team's anthropologist, inquired about ethnographic histories. The four met with village headmen and chatted with villagers about farming and banking. They considered how to select villages and ecological regions within the targeted provinces. Could their planned experiment work?

At the end of the Isan trip, Townsend asked Khun Sombat to take the first step. Could he organize practice pretests for the surveys? Through connections at various Thai universities, Townsend and Khun Sombat hoped to recruit a staff of graduate student researchers who had experience with nongovernmental organizations (NGOs).

Together with graduate students Anna Paulson and Tae Jeong Lee, Townsend had been working diligently in Chicago preparing questions to be tested. They had started with key theoretical concepts. Then they created summaries of articles on a range of topics, such as occupation choice, and compiled lists of key variables such as credit, savings, and talent. Not wanting to overlook other potentially relevant information, Paulson and Lee pondered World Bank studies and Indonesian family life surveys. Townsend sent the resultant questions, section by section, to Khun Sombat.

When the day came to pilot the surveys in early 1996, about 20 Bangkok graduate students with brief training under their belts piled into a bus headed for the poor, remote province of Sisaket. Paulson and Lee came along to observe.

Khun Sombat had translated Townsend's initial survey into Thai and arranged meetings with village headmen he knew from his work at BAAC. When the group arrived at its first stop, the little village of Bankasay, they met with the headman to arrange home stays and interview schedules with local families. Work began the next day. Enumerators fanned out in groups of two to visit households, banks, and community finance groups.

It was painfully slow going at first. As they moved from interview to interview, village to village, the TFRP team ran into suspicion, resistance, misunderstanding, and frustration. Some interviewees worried the information they gave would be used by the government to tax them. Others did not understand definitions such as that of a business, which they took to imply only something on scale with a factory or large corporation. Why, some asked, were there so many questions? The household survey had more than 250 detailed questions, and the financial institutions survey ran up to 400 pages.

With patient diplomacy and careful explanations, enumerators eased the suspicions of the respondents. They referred to a manual Khun Sombat had written about how to make introductions and how to explain the project. They assured nervous interviewees that information would be kept confidential. It was a process they would repeat for weeks, spending two or three days in a village before moving on, covering nine villages in four provinces—with several days of break in between—over two months.

This pilot phase showed that enumerators needed explanations and reassurances, too. Without sophisticated backgrounds in economics, they did not always understand the questions they were asking. After working all day until about eight in the evening, they would commiserate and try to help each other over dinner and then late into the night. With help from regular email contact with Townsend, they began to rephrase some of the problematic questions, work more efficiently, and get a better grip on the survey in general. Gradually, they began to boil it down from two to three days of work per household to two to three hours.

In the months that followed, Townsend looked over the pretest results with growing concern. Indications of economic disparity—in education, income, financial services—were everywhere. This seemed to match up with Townsend's earlier analysis of federal survey data. Townsend's observations didn't exist alone. A conference at the Thailand Development Research Institute (TDRI) in late 1993 had also noted the growing inequality among Thai citizens, amid industrialization and globalization.[2]

In October 1996, Townsend and Khun Sombat went to the national finance office, the Bank of Thailand, and various universities to present their analysis. When presenting the survey's initial findings, they noted that Thailand's record growth appeared to have left behind large segments of the population, making the economic gains unstable. Federal surveys were limited in that they focused primarily on consumption and lacked theoretical underpinning. There was a subsequent need for clear analysis, Townsend and Khun Sombat argued.

When Townsend asked for help funding the baseline survey to come, he was greeted with polite applause. "A lot of people attended our presentations, but nobody listened," Khun Sombat recalls. Refusing to be deterred, Townsend and Khun Sombat continued onward in search of additional funding.

Fortunately, with pretest experience, well-documented results, and an organizational structure in hand, Townsend and Paulson, working with the National Opinion Research Center (NORC) at the University of Chicago, received their first relatively large grant from the National

Institute of Child Health and Human Development (NICHD) for research and field operations. Townsend had dispelled doubts that a theorist like him could successfully design and implement a survey. The stage was set for the baseline survey, often referred to as the Big Survey by Townsend and staff, in April 1997. The Big Survey was intended as a baseline for a subsequent, more detailed evaluation of a few, carefully selected villages. Townsend would wire the first installment of tens of thousands of dollars from NORC.

From the skeleton staff of 20, they would need to expand to more than 200. They would require the help of more than two dozen specially trained team leaders and field editors to oversee the work of a small army of enumerators (see table 1.2 for a full list of TFRP staff and responsibilities). Those who had been enumerators during the pretest, in addition to new fourth-year students at Thammasat, Chulalongkorn,

Table 1.2:
TFRP Responsibilities as of 2011

TFRP's **project director**, Khun Sombat Sakunthasathien, directs field operations associated with both the annual and monthly surveys. He coordinates operations from interviews to data entry and liaises with community leaders and institutions on the ground to ensure that data collection runs smoothly. He oversees TFRP's funding and accounting functions. He also collaborates extensively with Townsend, the principal investigator, and the research team.

The project employs two **survey supervisors**. The survey supervisors conduct retraining prior to each survey, especially when questions have been added. They document authorization from the district and village headmen, update information on all households that will be surveyed, act as coordinators to the headmen in the field, and check data from the field in advance to ensure its accuracy.

The project employs three **translators**. The translators are responsible for translating all open-ended responses in the monthly and annual surveys, including the enumerator notes; answers outside the questionnaire's scope; questions about respondents' opinions, activities, health symptoms, and diseases; and use of financial institutions. Approximately 25% of each survey needs to be translated.

The project employs four part-time **environmental enumerators**. The environmental enumerators are responsible for taking environmental measures in each village, including soil fertility measures, soil tension and moisturizer, water chemistry, pH, TDS (total dissolved solids) in the local canal, and rainfall.

The project employs four **field editors** and four **assistant field editors**. The field editors work to coordinate with supervisors in the field, correct the questionnaire, and complete the primary data check before sending the data to the head office. Also, the field editors are responsible for interviewing and hiring from 12 to 15 enumerators for each province.

TFRP employs hundreds of **enumerators**. These are the individuals responsible for implementing the survey in the field, visiting households and villages, and recording the responses.

and Kasetsart Universities, would become field editors and supervisors. Word went out to various universities, and applications began to pour in for the enumerator jobs.

In early 1997, as the baseline survey loomed, TFRP had an unwelcome surprise. Only four of the newly hired team leaders and field editors showed up for a planning meeting. The rest were close to graduation and were busy looking for full-time work in a lucrative labor market. The robust Thai economy had driven up wages, making it hard to hire and retain employees on a modest budget like TFRP's.

In the weeks before they were scheduled to start the baseline survey, Khun Sombat interviewed more than 300 enumerator applicants, many university students; shifted staff to fill spaces; and managed to hire 16 new supervisors. Many of the new hires, working for university credit and 250 baht (about 7.50 USD) per completed survey, had little experience with economic theory or sociology. To familiarize themselves with the survey and the process involved, the new staff of roughly 240 set out for a final test run in mid-March, the start of the two-month university break. They got on chartered buses for Petchaburi, the same province Townsend and Khun Sombat had visited two years earlier.

Khun Sombat's old mentor, former development officer Pinitchai Sawat, smoothed the way. Pinitchai had written to local officials and colleagues in development offices asking for their help with the project.

Over the course of five days, the teams of enumerators and supervisors repeated the pretest formula, meeting with village headmen for initial planning and canvassing households and financial institutions. Local development officers introduced them to villagers.

At night, the young enumerators slept on mats at a monastery and a community development department office, their colorful sarongs hanging on laundry lines. They lived on a shoestring budget of 200 baht (about 6 USD) per person per day for everything but travel and lodging.

At the end of the Petchaburi test, field editors and other supervisors, including Khun Sombat and Townsend, met in Bangkok. Significant issues remained. Enumerators still struggled with the meanings behind some questions. For example, they did not understand whether "in the last year" meant the last twelve months or within the last calendar year, and they were confused by the coding system for some answers. Extensive conversations with the surveyors allowed the team to address problems early on and avoid having them surface after the survey was already in the field.

In the few weeks between the Petchaburi pre-test and the baseline survey, administrators revised questions, tweaked codebooks—the answer key where verbal responses were given alphanumeric variables, or codes—and updated manuals. Field editors did more training with enumerators in Bangbuatong District close to Bangkok, collecting and processing information while smoothing out the bumps.

The baseline survey was a few weeks away.

2   The Baseline Survey: 60,000 Questions in Two Months

In northeastern Thailand, the Mun River valley still retains the aura of the ancient Khmer Kingdom to which it belonged. The ruins of thousand-year-old temples rise up from the landscape, knotted tree trunks and heavy moss framing the weathered stone faces of gods and demons. The people of this remote, rural area still share dialects and beliefs with their cousins in neighboring Cambodia. Some still measure time by the distant drums of serene monasteries.

In Sisaket Province, paved roads and gas-powered farm tractors did not appear in some parts until the 1990s. It was not long ago that tiger paw marks dotted forest trails; medicine was a matter of roots and herbs; light came from coconut leaf torches; communal labor was repaid in whiskey, food, rice, or labor exchanges; and the only insurance policies were a water buffalo that could be sold or family members who could be relied upon in hard times. The name of one village, Sam Kha, or "Three Legs," recalls a time when villagers set forest traps to disable and capture elephants.

An ancient animism shapes the seasons for some villagers. At planting time, they implore the spirits with whiskey, a sacrificed chicken, candles, delicate cloth, bowls of homemade candies and betel nuts, cigarettes, and small boats with figures at the bow and stern. Shredded rice is offered before the harvest, flowers and sweets for the earth mother when storing the rice crop.

The spirits have not always responded. The memory of famine is fresh for some of the gray-haired villagers here, along with the desperation of those times that led to the theft of cattle and crops. But life is mostly peaceful now. Cranes and egrets stalk across the surface of endless rice paddies.

Figure 2.1, a map of Thailand, shows Sisaket and the three other provinces where the TFRP baseline survey was originally conducted— Buriram, Lop Buri, and Chachoengsao.

Figure 2.1
Map of Thailand

Sisaket

In March 1997, three double-decker buses drove into Sisaket, the first of four provinces where households would be interviewed. Each was loaded with about 70 TFRP enumerators, field editors, and supervisors, most of them in their early 20s.

They had started out from Bangkok that morning. It was spring break week for university students around the country, and there was an atmosphere of vacation-like adventure on the air-conditioned buses that buzzed with singing and boisterous joking. Hollywood movies played on televisions above the reclining seats, and Thai pop music wafted from radios. Some of the young women occasionally consulted the bulky cosmetic boxes they had brought.

After 10 hours and hundreds of miles of bad roads, the mood quieted. When the buses reached their destination in Sisaket, the students piled out, looking with uncertainty into the descending darkness.

Khun Sombat had smoothed the way as much as possible by contacting local officials in every target village of Sisaket and the three provinces to follow—an approach that would remain a key component of TFRP for years to come.

The governor of Phuket, Yuwat Wutthimethi, was instrumental to this outreach. He was the former head of the Ministry of the Interior's CDD and a respected mentor of Khun Sombat from his days with the BAAC. Weeks earlier, Yuwat had hosted his former protégé at his house for several days. The two discussed TFRP over dinner every night, where Yuwat expressed admiration for the ambitious plan.

Yuwat volunteered to call the governors of each of the target provinces to explain the project and secure their support. He arranged for meetings in which Khun Sombat would outline the survey's goals for the governors. In turn, the governor of each province would call on village officials to attend Khun Sombat's presentations at various community centers throughout the region. TFRP would pay for their transportation and provide lunch. All the officials had to do was to listen.

Khun Sombat pitched the survey as an educational project for the student surveyors. There would be 12 teams, he explained, each consisting of 11 enumerators, two field editors, a team leader, and a supervisor. Each team would have 10 days to canvas 60 households in a particular *tambon* before moving on to the next locale. Altogether, their goal was to visit almost 3,000 households in 200 villages.

Box 2.1
Rice Banks

A rice bank makes loans in the form of rice to be consumed. Those
households or members participating in the rice bank are usually
required to deposit or donate a given amount of rice at the founding of
the bank to build an initial fund. Rice banks are usually concentrated in
the more rural provinces. Buffalo banks are similar in nature with livestock being the form of currency.

They would also interview a total of 192 village headmen or key
informants, 262 officials from joint liability groups of the BAAC, and
161 representatives of village-level financial institutions, such as production credit groups, local rice banks, poverty eradication funds,
women's savings groups, and buffalo banks. Finally, they would take
soil and water samples at 10 of every 15 households interviewed per
village—1,920 in all. Soil collectors would photograph these plots in
three directions and record crop types and fertilizer use during the
previous five years. Field editors and supervisors would pore over the
survey results looking for missing data.

Names would be kept confidential, Khun Sombat promised. The
information would be used for academic purposes only. No one would
see higher taxes or government scrutiny as a result.

The headmen were convinced and agreed to take TFRP supervisors
for tours of their villages, making introductions along the way and
arranging interview schedules with households randomly selected
from an official CDD randomized list. They would draw up area maps
to help enumerators find their way. But maps alone would not be enough
to guide enumerators through the experiences that awaited them.

While relationship building with the community leaders was well
underway, the initial connections with households provided additional
hurdles. Due to limited telephone coverage, not knowing phone
numbers of existing phone lines, and certainly no email, TFRP relied
on postal mail and in-person conversations to make the appropriate
introductions. While the community leaders, whose relationships
proved vital, were on board with the project, some had not yet con-
tacted the households by the time the team arrived. This resulted in
enumerators spending more time than expected making introductions
and explaining the survey before conducting the interview. Moreover,
finding time needed for follow-up also proved difficult, as the com-

munities had long distances between them and transportation was not ideal.

TFRP approached the problem of connecting with households from two angles. First, the survey team (field editors and enumerators) utilized ethnographic mapping, which placed and labeled key sites that were important to the villages' history, culture, or the ecology of the area, building upon the work started by Alan Kolata. The maps also included the locations of households and other structures, many of which did not have recognized physical addresses. This way, instead of relying on verbal descriptions of locations from locals, sometimes puzzling to newcomers, the team had a central location where they could reference how to find the household they were set to interview.

In addition to locating the households, the teams had to grow accustomed to a bit of culture shock. Because the team was made up of members from mostly densely populated areas, enumerators were sometimes unaware of the caveats of rural agricultural life. To remedy this, TFRP also included a crop calendar and an occupational activity chart so that the team could understand the seasonal ebb and flow of the harvest as well as the characteristics of each worker's responsibilities. These combined efforts led to better coordination with the households and eased the arranging and executing of interviews.

The days began around seven. Riding in the back of a hired pickup, on a shared motorbike, or in a cart attached to a walking tractor, enumerators made their way to the households on their lists.

After they introduced themselves as politely as possible—being sure to show respect by using honorifics such as "grandfather" and "uncle"—enumerators explained the project, answered any questions, and eased lingering concerns. Curious children, friends, and neighbors often stood by and listened. While some households were skeptical at first, few refused to answer questions after listening to the enumerators' reassuring answers. After some small talk about the weather, the age of the house, or, perhaps, a child's cute smile, the interview began in earnest.

The baseline survey household questionnaire was divided into 22 sections, ranging from questions about family members' names to hypothetical questions about where to go for emergency funds. Using a coding system developed during the pretest surveys, enumerators entered most answers according to a corresponding number or letter. But before the answer could be coded, enumerators had to learn how to ask questions.

Open-ended questions about topics such as the best and worst crop years, which allowed interviewees to answer subjectively in their own words, seemed an ideal way to ease into the survey. As the farmer, barber, or shopkeeper began speaking more comfortably, enumerators often shifted to more intricate follow-up questions. Sensitive issues, such as savings and loans, had to be approached with care. Some interviewees, especially the more affluent relative to their neighbors, were tentative in discussing their finances. When faced with a suddenly taciturn interviewee, enumerators learned to change the subject to something lighter, returning to the matter later.

Not all respondents were so reserved about their finances. For instance, while discussing her household's savings, the wife of a retired army colonel saw fit to show proof. To the enumerator's surprise, she excused herself and then returned to the room with a box filled with gold jewelry and other valuables.

Certain sections seemed to impede enumerators and their interviewees more often than others. A module addressing cultivation covering so many details—from preferred fertilizer brands to crop storage techniques—became especially tedious.

The interviews themselves occasionally went off course unexpectedly. Some enumerators later told stories of showing up at the appointed time only to find the head of the household drunk and combative. At least one female enumerator was propositioned. Interviewees sometimes grew impatient with the process and expressed irritation. Enumerators specially trained to conduct financial institution surveys found little use for their accounting knowledge with a few community groups who kept poor records. The head of one farmers' savings and loan group claimed he could not locate any records.

Over time, enumerators learned to deal with obstacles using a blend of diplomacy, improvisation, patience and, perhaps most importantly, a good sense of humor.[1] If the atmosphere did not lend itself to a productive interview, they might reschedule and visit a nearby target household instead. Taking the time to allay an interviewee's concerns and to stress confidentiality of responses was essential. Also essential was thinking on the fly, diverting attention during tense or otherwise uncomfortable moments. While staying on schedule was important, time often allowed for breaks that helped to ease the mood or for repeat visits to gather complete information.

Beyond the unfamiliar geography, enumerators found themselves in new milieus both socially and culturally. For some accustomed to city life, adjusting to the rural atmosphere was difficult. In some places, they had to bathe in shrimp ponds. Meals could be modest, little more than rice and vegetables, and beds were generally mats on the floor. TFRP teams of 15 lived in small houses, dilapidated school buildings, and community health centers, often sharing a single bathroom. In fact, a nighttime bathroom visit might require a 500-meter walk. Afraid of ghosts, enumerators in one village chose to crowd into one room at an old temple, rather than risk sleeping separately.

With the help of consulting professors from Chiang Mai University, the young enumerators learned a great deal about the customs and dialects of the regions they visited. In the northeastern Isan region, where Townsend had traveled in early days of formulating the survey, they were told it was impolite to directly refuse a drink in the evening. Instead, they should refer to some imagined malady that prevented them from drinking and stress that they would otherwise gladly accept the offer. Male enumerators were told that coming on to local girls was a surefire way to court community disapproval. Playing guitar or singing with friends was fine, but to be kept at an appropriate volume.

Many of the responses from the villagers were surprising, eye-opening, and inspiring. In one village, a poor family offered their entire house to the enumerators as a respite, decamping for several days to a nearby friend's dwelling. In another poor village, almost every resident turned out to bid farewell to enumerators with a traditional Lao celebration, honoring the enumerators with chanting, a presentation of string amulets, and a feast of curry chicken, fried fish, papaya salad, and sticky rice.

Buriram

The TFRP staff caravan made its way west from Sisaket to Buriram, Khmer for "city of happiness." Like Sisaket, the province had once been part of the Khmer Empire, with ruins from that era and dormant volcanoes scattered across the landscape, and most of Buriram's residents lived modestly. The elderly among them recalled schools without books, where wood from the *Bombax ceiba* (cotton tree) served as a slate and limestone chunks doubled as writing instruments. They told enumerators of times when food was so scarce that people felt fortunate to have diseased meat. In the past, farmers unaware of or unable to afford pesticides implored rice borers, an insect pest, to leave their crops while burning joss sticks (incense) in banana leaf cones.

It was the dry season when the double-decker buses pulled into Buriram. Severe drought in Cambodia had driven factions of various armed groups over the border, including remnants of the Khmer Rouge and its splinter groups. There had been many reports of violent robberies in the *tambon* of Nong Mai Ngam, and some TFRP staff felt apprehensive.

At Khun Sombat's request, the nearby border patrol district office sent four rangers to escort enumerators in Nong Mai Ngam. Khun Sombat paid the soldiers, armed with semi-automatic rifles and shotguns, a per diem and provided their meals. He asked that they keep a comfortable distance and wear casual clothing, jeans, and T-shirts, so as not to scare the villagers.

Even though the staff felt more at ease, the security precautions did little to speed up interviews. In some villages, many of the interviewees were elderly people who spoke primarily Khmer. Anticipating this problem, TFRP had hired local enumerators who spoke the dialect. But the elderly posed a specific challenge. Enumerators would dutifully record any words they could not fully understand, and then consult village headmen or others for translations. The process made for long days that began shortly after dawn and often did not end until after eight at night. Survey teams took a day to review and edit their data after visiting each *tambon*. But the break from interviewing did little to ease growing stress.

As the buses continued west into Lop Buri, a province of rich alluvial plains and green hills, staff tensions began to flare.

Profile: Bui

Among the pre-test veterans that baseline survey enumerators turned to for guidance was Laddawan "Bui" Kamkoh, a 34-year-old former Thai Army Ranger with a jokester streak. With her boyish haircut, baggy jeans, and polo shirts, Bui seemed to be everywhere at once, chatting with villagers, cracking jokes with children, and making the rounds with sometimes-overwhelmed enumerators.

As a young girl, Bui had listened with rapt attention as her older brothers recalled their military exploits. She had joined straight out of high school, but quickly distinguished herself as a different kind of soldier. For most of her seven years as a ranger, she had worked with Cambodian refugees along the border, taking time off to earn a degree in library science.

Box 2.2
Refugees Residing in Thailand

Having not borne the costs of the Vietnam War, as did Vietnam and Laos, or civil war, as did Myanmar (formerly Burma) and Cambodia, Thailand emerged from the 20th century in a different developmental capacity than its eastern and western neighbors. Thailand, however, has not been immune to the calamity of human conflict. Some 150,000 documented Burmese refugees live in nine camps operated in western Thailand, and 70,000 additional unregistered Burmese refugees live outside of the official camps. Prior to their repatriation to Laos in 2009, northern Thailand was home to 4,000 Hmong Lao refugees.

It became clear she was not well suited for army life. She would break out of the ranger encampment at night to go drinking with friends in town. TFRP provided an intriguing alternative, a chance to travel and pursue more intellectual work. After hearing about the project from a university friend in 1996, Bui marched into Khun Sombat's Bangkok office and stood at attention. "My name is Bui," she said, "and I want to work for you."

With her fluent Khmer and easy-going aura, Bui presented an image of hard-working stability and fun-loving playfulness. A natural communicator, Bui was adept at maintaining local relations and taming staff tensions. In the weeks remaining, the success of the baseline survey would hinge on Bui's ability to maintain morale in the face of culture shock and personal conflicts.

Lop Buri

The team traveled next to Lop Buri, a past provincial capital for the Khmer Empire. For a brief period in the 17th century, the province became the seat of power for the Ayutthaya Kingdom's western-looking ruler, Narai the Great, who employed French architects to build his palace. Known in legend as the home of the monkey god Hanuman, Lop Buri's provincial capital is a primate's paradise. Bold and brazen, monkeys wander the streets unmolested and enjoy a feast in their honor every November.

Although the province had an alluring exotic nature about it, a dispute among one team was shaping up to be the baseline survey's first significant conflict. Several enumerators thought their field editor had been too harsh in dealing with their mistakes. As payback, they had slipped into one of his meals a mild medication that brought on diarrhea. Recriminations became more heated.

Moving quickly to head off further deterioration of relations between the field editor and the enumerators, Bui stepped in. She called the team to a meeting and asked for both sides of the story. Without threatening punishment, Bui made clear that a fundamental line had been crossed. It was time to set aside differences, she said. She made the case that the project and its ambitious goals were bigger than any individual disagreement and too important to be compromised by pettiness. There was only one more province left, and it was essential that everyone pull together. They did not have to like each other, but they would have to work together, Bui said sternly. Focus on what this survey can accomplish, she urged, not just your personal issues.

Unfortunately, the team's supervisor quickly unraveled Bui's effort at reconciliation. He presented the team with a form. If you want to quit, the supervisor told the enumerators, sign the form. Five of the twelve signed and left the project shortly thereafter. Scrambling, Bui had to reform the team with the remaining seven enumerators and five more borrowed from other groups.

In a sense, TFRP had been lucky to avoid any other major flare-ups so far. After all, the more than 200 staff members had been working, living, and traveling together in sometimes strained conditions for almost two months. Fatigue made some enumerators grow impatient as the survey's conclusion drew nearer.

Then, in mid-April, just before the buses were set to leave for the last province, Chachoengsao, TFRP's leader was called away suddenly.

Khun Sombat's 83-year-old father had died in his sleep. Rushing back to his home outside Bangkok, Khun Sombat arrived in the night. Assuming the traditional role of the family's eldest child, he carried his father's body down from the second floor of the old teak house.

During the next seven nights, hundreds of friends, family, and colleagues poured into the house to pay their respects to the widely esteemed former national revenue department official. On the eighth day, Khun Sombat led a procession with his father's body to a nearby temple and donated to local schools all of the nearly 200,000 baht (about 6,000 USD) his family had received as gifts. Because of his busy schedule with TFRP, it would be two years—one year longer than tradition dictates—before Khun Sombat would scatter his father's ashes in a Bangkok river near his childhood home.

Sobered, Khun Sombat rejoined the staff on the last leg of its trip. He was in for an unpleasant surprise.

Chachoengsao

Without their leader for the previous week, TFRP staff had been anchorless. Previously muted disagreements and resentments had come to a head in the survey's last stop, the urbanized Chachoengsao Province, 80 kilometers from Bangkok. Without an established mediation system, some supervisors had found no resolution for their disagreements. Bickering among some enumerators—over relationships and food, among other things—grew bitter. Bui and other peacekeepers had trouble keeping up. Nerves were frayed.

Two groups in particular seemed to have intractable conflicts: Ill will remained over the food poisoning incident, and disagreements over a pay schedule had estranged one team's field editor from his staff. Enumerators in that group were demanding regular payments instead of work-based compensation. This field editor argued that standardized pay would lead to sloppy and incomplete surveys.

Sensing an endangerment of the future of the project, Khun Sombat met with the supervisors and then the field editors and enumerators of each of the two distressed teams. He spoke calmly in measured tones. "Our work with this project is nearly done," he told them. "You and I have come a long way and accomplished a great deal. It has been my honor to work with you, and I do not blame you if you want to leave now. If everyone decides together that is their wish, I will postpone the survey rather than continue under a cloud of misunderstanding." But, Khun Sombat added, "I ask that you delay your decision for three days."

During that time, the survey halted. Khun Sombat reserved dozens of rooms at a modest hotel back in Lop Buri. Enumerators, field editors, and supervisors could relax, sleep in a comfortable bed, take a hot shower, and enjoy each other's company without work pressures.

If the two problematic teams decided against continuing, Khun Sombat figured he would return to Chachoengsao in coming weeks with a group of supervisors and team leaders. It would not be ideal, but it would work, he hoped.

In the meantime, Khun Sombat resolved to appoint a temporary director if he ever had to leave the project again. Whether the two teams resigned or not, he had gained crucial experience and better understood the dynamics of managing and inspiring a team. He recognized the importance of familial bonds and open lines of communication among staff. It was essential, he now understood, to intervene early in brewing conflicts and to coordinate management strategies in order to avoid temper flare ups and keep things running smoothly. It had been a turning point for TFRP, Khun Sombat, and his staff.

At the end of three days together in the Lop Buri hotel, before returning to Chachoengsao, Khun Sombat reminded the two teams he had spoken to earlier that they were free to quit.

No one left.

Enumerators collect soil samples as part of the baseline survey, which ultimately collected samples from more than 1,920 individual plots across Thailand.

A group of young enumerators gather at TFRP's offices. To recruit the more than 200 enumerators needed for the baseline survey, TFRP worked with several universities in Thailand to advertise positions for students.

A large group of enumerators and TFRP staff attend a training session prior to the baseline survey. Training sessions such as this provide an opportunity for staff to discuss common mistakes, clarify the intent of certain questions, and learn how to be more efficient.

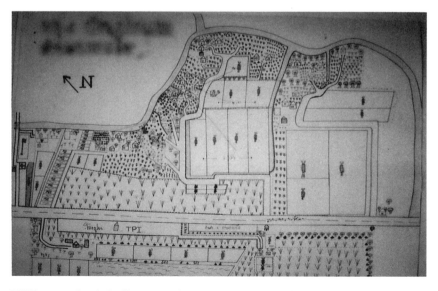

TFRP creates detailed village maps that give enumerators information on the survey area, including the location of households and land use by crop type.

A TFRP staff member in the Sisaket Province reviews survey data in 2011. Field editors and supervisors read over the completed answer booklets to ensure the accuracy of the data collected. Photo: Natalie Hoover El-Rashidy.

Khun Sombat addresses TFRP staff at a training session in the early years of the survey. Under his leadership, TFRP has grown to more than 70 employees spread across a central office and four field outposts.

Townsend visits northern Thailand in 1993, just before meeting Khun Sombat for the first time in Chiang Mai. Townsend had been conducting informal field research on village economies.

A rice farmer demonstrates the use of an iron buffalo, or two-wheeled tractor, in harvesting rice. The Townsend Thai surveys track ownership of machines like this, since they typically represent a large investment for many Thai families.

3   The Annual Resurveys: The Financial Crisis and Beyond

In July 1997 the lights went out in Thailand.

It had been two months since the baseline survey. After weeks of combing through answer sheets, Khun Sombat was preparing to mail the final data to Chicago. It was, he thought, the end of TFRP.

Then, grim headlines began marching across morning papers. Panic spread. The government left intense market speculation and a ballooning foreign debt unchecked, leading to a sudden, massive devaluation of the Thai baht. In the days that followed the devaluation, the Tom Yam Kung Crisis, named for a famous Thai shrimp soup, began in Thailand and spread throughout eastern Asia. It drove down currencies (see figure 3.1), devalued markets, and put millions out of work. South Korea's stock market, a juggernaut for decades, saw record drops. Economic unrest and rioting in Indonesia forced out the long-reigning dictator, Suharto, in May 1998. In Thailand, the baht lost half its value and the suicide rate tripled.

Box 3.1
The 1997 Asian Financial Crisis

> After 1997, Thailand experienced the full brunt of the Asian financial crisis. The baht, which had formerly been pegged to a basket of currencies including the US dollar, was devalued significantly. At the peak of the crisis, the Thai stock market dropped 75 percent. Thailand relied upon the World Bank and the International Monetary Fund for emergency bailout funds during the crisis. The fallout from (and on-going recovery of) the Asian financial crisis is seen in the data collected during the Townsend Thai Project.

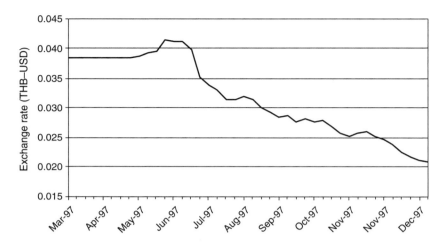

Figure 3.1
Devaluation of the Thai Baht

Crisis to Opportunity

Townsend began to realize in October 1997 that the crisis would present a unique opportunity. In the baseline survey's data, TFRP had an important benchmark. Against it, they could measure the financial meltdown's long-term impact. How would average families and businesses be affected? How would they respond? He called Khun Sombat. Would he consider doing a resurvey?

Within days, Townsend was on a plane to Thailand. There was no money yet for the resurvey, and the financial dynamic of Thailand was changing rapidly. Time was not on their side.

Townsend's concern with time and money changed over a buffet lunch. Townsend and Khun Sombat had arranged the lunch meeting at a trendy downtown Bangkok hotel to discuss funding with a Ford Foundation representative. She had told them that Thailand was "growing up," and the foundation no longer saw a role for itself there. Within a matter of weeks, Ford would be moving its offices to Vietnam. While the resurvey sounded worthwhile, the Ford representative said, the foundation generally did not support research work of any kind, preferring to focus on healthcare pilot projects. Could Townsend and Khun Sombat put together a proposal with an eye toward health and education issues?

The two men rushed back to Khun Sombat's office, where they spent the next three days composing a 12-page proposal in between meals at a noodle shop next door. Khun Sombat and Townsend linked their economic study—a planned annual resurvey—to nationwide health and well-being issues. They would look at year-to-year changes, charting how people dealt with risk and uncertainty in the wake of the financial crisis. They would return to the same provinces surveyed in the baseline but reduce the number of target villages from 192 to 64 and the number of households from 2,880 to 960. The focus for eventual analysis: primarily poor, rural communities most vulnerable to economic upheaval and policy shifts.

The timing was perfect, Khun Sombat and Townsend argued. The resurvey presented a manageable way to link micro- and macroeconomic theory. The circumstances were historic, and the potential for profound socioeconomic understanding unprecedented. By the end of the week, Ford had pledged 60,000 USD. The foundation's Bangkok office was shuttered permanently two weeks later.

The Resurvey

Townsend and Khun Sombat set about modifying the baseline survey questionnaire. Questions regarding income, consumption, assets, borrowing, lending, and the like would remain essentially the same. Unlike the baseline survey, however, their focus would not be on the past five years, but only the past 365 days and any changes from the previous year.

Also, beginning in the second year, they would look carefully at household businesses through the prism of a new battery of questions. In all other respects, the resurvey would be a simpler, less-detailed version of the baseline survey. Like the first study, the resurvey would target households, village headmen, and local financial institutions. For simplicity, BAAC groups were initially left out because the baseline survey data on the matter seemed sufficient.

Khun Sombat began putting together teams. He needed 60 people, including field editors. With help from enumerators who stayed on after the baseline survey, Khun Sombat recruited at satellite campuses of Rajabhat University. He found eager students fluent in Lao, Khmer, Sui, and various local dialects. After a week of training at the central office and a week of field training, the new teams, led by baseline survey veterans, were ready to go.

In early 1998, Khun Sombat accompanied team leaders to various local organizations in the target provinces where he showed, by example, how to begin survey work. Many of the officials were familiar with Khun Sombat from the baseline survey. They welcomed him back with smiles and jokes, curious to hear about baseline survey data and his plans for the new survey.

Khun Sombat was thorough in his explanations, patient with questions, and solicitous of individual concerns. He asked for help in contacting households and arranging interviews. At the end of these presentations, he provided a free lunch for all who listened.

By the spring of 1998, it was time to get to work. It promised to be a hectic year without holiday for Khun Sombat. Not only did he have the resurvey ahead, but also he would have to simultaneously arrange a pre-test of the monthly survey Townsend was busy formulating, according to their earlier rigorous evaluation plans.[1]

Equipped with information from the baseline survey, four teams fanned out to the target provinces in April. Each team—12 enumerators, a field editor, and an assistant editor—would go from *tambon* to *tambon*. While editors would work at temporary offices in central villages, enumerators would travel from village to village, house to house, over the next six weeks. Local headmen would arrange for their lodging in the often remote, poor communities along the way.

Like their baseline survey predecessors, most enumerators were 20-something students short on experience but with much energy and enthusiasm. Unlike the baseline survey teams, resurvey teams had the advantage of experience. Some baseline survey supervisors became field editors for the resurvey, providing invaluable perspective and insight for new enumerators.

Field editors stayed in centralized towns poring over data at temporary offices because many roads in the target areas made for rough and time-consuming travel. Despite the logistical hurdles, field editors managed to impart guidance to enumerators who stopped by with stacks of answer sheets and piles of questions. The conflicts and complaints—from both enumerators and target households—that tinged the end of baseline survey largely evaporated in the resurvey's early days.

Every week that first year, supervisors from the four teams would meet in a central place to discuss issues and questions that arose. While the baseline survey experience ensured fewer major mistakes, plenty of smaller quandaries surfaced. They were reflected in emails from the teams to Anna Paulson, now the vice president and director of financial research at the Federal Reserve Bank of Chicago, who had helped formulate the resurvey questionnaire.

How, enumerators asked Paulson, should they record fruit trees grown for household consumption as opposed to sale? It's not always clear whether the cycle of planting, growing, and harvesting is complete, they pointed out. Should they create a new code (every survey answer had a corresponding data entry code) for gift expenditures, such as money given for a monk's ordination? What about families that said in the census they were separate households yet always ate and worked together?

Answering these and other similar questions required balancing many factors, as the procedures followed in the survey would impact not only the accuracy and interpretation of data derived from the surveys but also the time that it would take to do the interviews. The process of gathering data tested the patience of both the enumerators and the survey households. Occasionally, economic theory provided a clear answer to the question: for example, families that pool resources and always eat and work together could be thought of as a single household.

But other times, the "correct" answer depended on how one imagined the data might be used in the future. For example, if the priority was to establish an accurate measure of household wealth, then clearly the answer to the fruit tree question would be important. If fruit trees grown for household consumption were ignored, then households with these assets would seem to be "poorer" than they really were. Another possibility was to ask enumerators to keep track of the extent to which fruit was used for household consumption versus sold.

While keeping track of everything seemed like an appealing solution, it was obvious that it could become unwieldy. More generally, it could compromise the quality of the data. If every potential ambiguity added new questions to the survey instrument, it eventually would become too long and too complicated, which could increase errors and possibly decrease participation. So meeting the needs of future researchers had to be done with questions about feasibility in mind: What will be easiest for enumerators to do? Is this a big deal or not? Is it 0.5 percent of households who have fruit trees for household consumption or 10 percent? Answering these questions subsequently determined procedures for enumerators and led to refining the questionnaire. Data reliability, knowledge of the context in which the enumerators were working, economic theory, and statistics all had to be combined with common sense to come up with workable solutions.

Paulson's replies to the various quandaries were often leavened with subtle humor. In response to a woman who considered her family's accounts balanced, despite debts left by a philandering husband, Paulson was sanguine: "The key thing is what the wife thinks."

There was sometimes confusion over converting, say, a coconut harvest into kilograms. "I think that you should decide on your own what an appropriate conversion rate for coconuts to kilograms is, and you should use it," wrote Paulson.

With measurement being such an important aspect of the surveys, TFRP soon realized such problems would occur frequently, especially given the diverse regions they surveyed. Any accepted conversion would not only need to be considered thoroughly but also communicated to the other teams elsewhere so as to standardize the results. The field supervisors were assigned the task of going between each area and communicating the method of measurement. Any time they were uncertain, they would appeal to Paulson for her advice.

TFRP subsequently published a reference/conversion guide where all measurements not easily conceived in a standard measurement, like kilograms, could be referenced for conversion purposes. The guide also included vocabulary used for plants, objects, and activities. The entire document was continually updated and placed in each survey team's interview manual. Also, the field supervisors held seminars for the survey team in each province, allowing TFRP employees to exchange anecdotes and solutions to problems that arose.

Where there was room to expand definitions, Paulson encouraged it. Where a more thorough approach to questions was warranted, she urged it. More than a few times, field editors sent enumerators to re-do interviews or to follow up on incomplete or unclear responses.

Lessons learned in the field were also codified, and an ask-and-check control system with the central office in Bangkok, and on occasion Chicago, was also institutionalized. The system essentially involved back-and-forth communication between the central office and the field that allowed for the questionnaire to be adapted and standardized. For example, if enumerators noticed patterns in responses (such as wanting to respond with "large amount" or "small amount" versus a numerical quantity on a particular question), they first had to contact Bangkok before recording it. The central office was responsible for making sure all responses were recorded in such a way that the data could later be used for study (e.g., saying 15 kilos as opposed to "a large amount"). The central office also assured that if any response adaptations were accepted, they were properly codified and all changes were disseminated to all field offices, further standardizing the survey.

As time went on, the stream of questions thinned. Enumerators were learning how to minimize errors and apply lessons learned to slightly modified circumstances. They talked among themselves about maintaining eye contact during interviews, despite any boredom or fatigue. They knew it was best to avoid interjecting or rushing an answer. They understood the importance of gentle diplomacy.

Once the interview had taken place, the records were sent to TFRP's central office just outside of Bangkok for processing. From the beginning, it was evident that transporting the records such a great distance was slowing error detection and correction. By the time the office in Bangkok communicated a probable error to the field office, the team had already moved onto another province. In order to follow up and correct the error, the team had to backtrack and again encountered some problems with making connections, since postal mail and in-person conversations were the norm. All of this led to much longer timeframes than anticipated.

To ease the strain, TFRP's central office sent five computers to each field office—bringing the total to seven at each location—for the period of the resurvey. Equipped with software specifically for entering survey data, the additional computers sped up the process significantly. The team could now spend two days interviewing in the community and one day verifying data or asking follow-up questions. This allowed the data to at least be assessed one time before the team relocated. Over time, field editors became more efficient at cross-checking recorded answers against baseline data and managing yearly logistics. Eventually, the teams got the timeframe of the annual resurvey down to an average of 16 days, spread over two months.

The resurvey initially overlooked information from the baseline survey. After several rounds of the annual resurvey, discrepancies in household answers became clear, however, and surveyors and field editors began consulting previous data. For example, households were asked about assets purchased or sold during the year and the assets they currently possessed. If those numbers did not line up with the previous year's tally, it triggered a red flag and follow-up questions.

This led to its own problems, as it became clear some enumerators regarded the previous data as reliable rather than using it as a tool in the new interviews. To deal with this, Khun Sombat restricted access to previous years' data to field editors.

Another change came in the amount of autonomy Khun Sombat gave to the field editors in running their field offices. Gradually, as experience grew and individual operations became smoother, TFRP's central office took a more hands-off approach to management. Senior staff members given some discretion and responsibility made better, more timely decisions.

As a result, the field offices—located in Chachoengsao, Lop Buri, Sisaket, and Buriram—adopted rules and schedules to fit particular conditions and staff needs so that resurvey data continued to be collected in timely and consistent ways. By adapting to local conditions and staffs, the survey was able to remain successful in diverse settings. This decentralized management structure has served TFRP well over the years, given the geographic spread of operations and increasing scope.

Other adaptations of the survey process had to do with how field editors monitored the enumerators' schedules and the quality of their surveys. While some offices enforced strict schedules, others could not because of the variable hours of enumerators' second jobs. Some field editors ratcheted up supervision to ensure on-time work, while others simply docked pay if enumerators made errors. To avoid complacency and the temptation to recycle old data, at least one field office had enumerators switch target households every year.

Khun Sombat encouraged field editors to share their experiences with each other during meetings he held at the central office every three months and to coordinate more regular phone calls among the field offices. Where he thought it potentially fruitful, Khun Sombat shared his own experiences too. He told field editors, for example, about how, as a BAAC credit officer, he had asked clients to stand in front of a Buddha image in his office and pledge to repay the loan. Repayment rates had skyrocketed, he recalled. Perhaps field editors could do something similar with their staff as a way to ensure careful work?

Eventually, each field office developed its own distinct personality and atmosphere. They ran the gamut from Lop Buri's laid-back rural headquarters in a family compound, complete with outdoor lounge area, hammocks, and wandering chickens, to Chachoengsao's concrete storefront office, an austere space that could double as an insurance agency. All of the field offices, however, were papered with maps and satellite images of the surrounding areas that showed target houses marked with yellow tape. Calculators and computers shared space with family portraits, plug-in stoves and, occasionally, children.

At least one of the offices seemed to have supernatural attributes. For several years, the Sisaket team made its office in a two-story building that some said was haunted. Neighbors said on several occasions they had seen a ghostly arm pushing the front door open from the inside, and staff members swore they could hear children playing on the empty second level. Finally, the field editor at the time tried to appease any restless spirits by making an offering at the building's spirit house, a small structure most Thai buildings have for the spirit of residents past. The haunting incidents stopped.

Profile: Lek

Still, the annual resurvey's tight timeline, villagers' unpredictable schedules, and other unforeseeable factors have made for more than a few problems. Easing such obstacles is the job of Thiptanradee "Lek" Punchayayodanlin, the resurvey's supervisor since 2004. Working primarily from the central office outside Bangkok, she manages the yearly endeavor with a mellow but firm approach that has won her colleagues' respect.

Growing up in Chonburri Province near the South China Sea, Lek had frequent bouts of dengue fever, a mosquito-borne illness. During the hospital stays that resulted, she became enamored of doctors and their art of healing power and aspired to become one herself. Although her dreams of a medical career cooled over time, Lek never lost her desire to change lives. At Thammasat University, she studied sociology and anthropology and, during vacations, helped build water supply systems and schools in poor communities. Her experience as an enumerator during the pre-test—riding a tractor from village to village across glisteningly beautiful paddy fields—had sold her on the project.

Lek demands respect, but gives it just as easily. She regularly checks in with and seeks the input of field editors and enumerators. This ensures not only consensus, but a tone of openness. Every year during the resurvey, Lek stays in touch with field editors, helping them replace target households that have moved and organizing workable interview schedules. Field editors call with issues ranging from a need for temporary staff housing in a remote area, to last-minute schedule overhauls, to female enumerators who feel intimidated by local toughs.

Lek is careful every year to reconnect and coordinate with local officials, presenting them with a letter from TFRP's main office shortly after New Year's. She visits again during the resurvey, always careful to show deference, and occasionally gives small gifts such as blankets or fruit.

Unlike government studies, which can result in increased funding for a certain area, local officials know the TFRP survey will bring no money to their village. These officials have no need to pretend to be enthusiastic about projects imposed on their community that may not actually be needed. They have no gain in overstating poverty or otherwise distorting answers, as there is no money coming anyway. Rather, it is emphasized from the outset that this is a study done by professors and students who are learning about rural life. Villagers hold teachers and students in great respect and are generous with their time. They even offer hospitality some can barely afford. Occasionally, local officials might ask for information about soil composition data or weather histories, but aside from these small curiosities, they never ask for any type of remuneration, which is a testament to Lek's diplomacy and the message TFRP brings to households.

Since assuming her role after a four-year stint as field editor in Sisaket Province, Lek has been in a unique position to see how the passage of time affects the resurvey's target households. She heard about the child in Chachoengsao who died of dengue fever, the same illness that plagued her as a girl. Ignorant of dengue's symptoms, the boy's parents had delayed going to a clinic because it was too far to travel for what they assumed was a common cold. There were the two elderly sisters in Sisaket. One was paralyzed, the other infirm. They survived on 300 baht (about 9 USD) a month in government aid. There was the old woman who lived alone and ate little more than soup made from water and the dried flowers she kept in a tin. More than half of the numerous chicken farms that once populated the countryside went out of business when egg prices dropped and avian flu caused a worldwide scare.

As the years passed and Thailand's economy rebounded, more of the stories Lek heard were about newfound wealth and improved quality of life. Using knowledge they had gleaned from agricultural television programs and government extension offices, farmers were experimenting with rice varieties and crop rotations. They had extra money to invest in second businesses and home renovations. Children could stay in school longer than their parents had. Rural roads were paved for the first time; motorbikes, cellular phones, and video stores were becoming common. In places such as remote Buriram near the Cambodian border, cellular towers were beginning to sprout among the rice, cassava, and sugarcane fields.

As the resurvey's makeup expanded, so did the staff. By 2000, the annual resurvey's third year, teams had gone from a mix of local staff and temporary outside hires who traveled among provinces to all local staff who worked from centralized offices. Most enumerators also worked on the monthly or micro surveys TFRP instituted shortly after the resurvey began. It meant more experience and more thorough data collecting for the study. It also meant extra income for the enumerators, who otherwise might have had little work during the relatively inactive dry season.

The survey project as a whole has and will continue to evolve. Coming years will likely bring more change to the resurvey. Considering the significant role of health and education in financial success, more questions on those topics are planned. Where do rural villagers find healthcare and how much do they spend on it? What has become of the young people who returned home with children to raise and few skills to market after the economic crisis? What effects will recent improvements in education levels among members of the workforce have?

The resurvey would not have a future were it not for an odd bit of irony. It owed its early survival to the 1997 financial crisis that had ravaged so many lives. At the time, the initial grant of 60,000 USD from the Ford Foundation had twice the buying power it would have had before the crisis. Intended to keep the resurvey afloat for one year, the grant kept the study solvent for more than two years before other funding sources became available. But, as is typical with large-scale surveys, ongoing money management can be arduous.

Both Townsend and Khun Sombat plan for unforeseen financial challenges, which inevitably come. They economize where possible, such as consolidating field visits to save on gas and turning off office air conditioning during lunch breaks. Traveling staff, regardless of seniority, receive the same modest per diems. They streamline and tweak survey operations to handle uneven and suspect funding amid US federal budget crises. They juggle staff payments and the survey's constant renewal with questions about when and how much money will materialize. It's a study of financial risk and uncertainty. It's also a study *in* financial risk and uncertainty.

One thing is certain: The annual surveys have provided an unprecedented look into how families deal with risk in their own lives, both financially and personally. Researchers who use the data are able to better understand how individuals and communities function, and 15 years of panel data from the same households has captured how families adapt to change and how household membership changes over time. TFRP sees children grow up and graduate, people migrate to other areas, workers retire, and children take on the care of their parents. Only a project with such longevity could provide a close study of people's lives as well as become an asset for future generations.

4 The Monthly Surveys

It was on the radio. It was on county government bulletin boards and the tips of local officials' tongues. Wanted: local residents with university degrees for part-time work; must have good interpersonal skills, strong work ethic, and sense of adventure. Length of employment: uncertain.

While managing the first annual resurvey in the spring of 1998, TFRP launched yet another survey, which would come to be the heart of the Thai Project vision. This questionnaire, to be administered monthly, promised a much more detailed, micro-level perspective on village-level family networks, markets, and formal credit and insurance institutions. The monthly survey was a laboratory for the ever-growing, ambitious scope of Townsend's research. The monthly survey would cover the same four provinces in the baseline survey—Chachoengsao, Lop Buri, Buriram, and Sisaket—though it would target different households.

Designing and assembling the questionnaires in Chicago was a mammoth undertaking. In the field, the survey would begin with extensive interviews for baseline data and then settle into detailed monthly overviews. The range of topics would cover crop operations, fish and shrimp businesses, shops, livestock, illness, formal and informal borrowing, lending, and gift giving. Respondents would have to distinguish animal stock from expenses and revenue flows. The costs and benefits of raising chickens, for example, were separated from the profit the birds' eggs brought when sold to local restaurants.

Professor Townsend used the expertise of the University of Chicago's National Opinion Research Center (NORC) to help develop a tracking system using rosters so that enumerators would know what topics previous interviews had covered and what topics remained to be explored. While enumerators would be returning to the same households each month, given the households' occupations, their activities might change from month to month. The survey developers had to anticipate that the content of the monthly survey would potentially change throughout the year. For example, additional questions about crop yield would need to be added for the months when crops were usually harvested. Anna Paulson and Townsend were consumed with inventing and reinventing these instruments.

A significant burden also fell on Khun Sombat. He and his staff would have to manage the hectic schedule coinciding with the resurvey. They would have to teach new enumerators the monthly survey's rhythms. Together, they would have to earn the trust and cooperation of households every month for the foreseeable future. For all involved, 1998 was a year of long hours and little rest.

Enumerator applications began to roll in for the planned monthly survey. They were from math teachers, rubber factory workers, traveling salesmen, clerks, and at least one beautician. The applicants had degrees in marketing, home economics, and even microbiology. They were attracted to the flexible hours and Saturdays off, unusual for Thai businesses. It was not a nine-to-five office job, and it would not require enumerators to move from their region. Previous experience had proven the wisdom of hiring staff within the region who spoke the dialect, though these staff could not live in the village where they worked (except for the data assessor and soil/water quality testers, who all lived in the communities where they worked) and were strictly forbidden from interviewing their own family and relatives. The enumerators would have time to study for advanced degrees, take care of their families' farms or shops, and look after their elderly parents.

Many of those signing the two-year contracts were unmarried women in their 20s with agricultural backgrounds. Thai culture dictated that they live with their parents until marriage. For some of these women, the survey jobs were an opportunity to get out of the house and interact with other educated young people. The extra income was also an incentive. To some enumerators whose family farms were facing drought, the salary would prove to be a lifeline.

Using the 1997 baseline survey, Townsend selected one *tambon* (from the original 12) per *changwat* in which randomly selected villages would have similar environmental conditions and significantly different economic institutions. Within each *tambon*, four nonadjacent villages were then selected.[1] This varied sampling facilitated Townsend's vision for an expanded monthly study on risk, insurance, and the family; the National Institute of Child Health and Human Development (NICHD) provided funding.

In each of the total 16 villages included in the monthly survey's scope, enumerators would interview 15 households from the baseline survey and 30 new households, bringing the total to 45 per village, and 720 in all. Soil and water samples would be taken at 10 sites from the baseline survey and 25 new sites, for a total of 35 sites per village, and 560 overall.

The Village Census

In the spring of 1998, a team of six TFRP veterans from the baseline survey went from *changwat* to *changwat* pre-testing questionnaires for the monthly survey to come. In the summer, armed with this training, the new enumerators spread out across the four target *changwats*.

First they had to describe the population in the villages being surveyed. At the time, government census reports were notoriously unreliable because of election-related manipulation, a lack of centralized data, and the absence of any incentive to report household changes. A single house in Lop Buri, for example, was listed in the official census as having 100 residents at one point. Unwilling to trust federal census data for this detailed village-level study, Khun Sombat ordered a thorough inventory of each village's structures and its inhabitants, if any. This accounting would also serve a new goal of Townsend's: identifying villagers who would likely make transactions with survey target households over subsequent interview months.

Working with headmen, enumerators sketched gridded maps of each community and then visited and painstakingly inventoried each structure—from rambling houses to tiny coal bunkers—assigning each a number according to its location. The 14th house in zone 2 of the map, for example, would be designated structure # 2014. They took copious notes. How many household members (people who sleep and eat there at least 15 days a month) resided there? What did each do for work?

Villagers wondered: Who were these young people traipsing around? Due to Khun Sombat's diplomacy, village headmen spread the word: nothing to fear.

With the census complete, enumerators visited each target household to collect baseline information, asking a range of historical questions about work, family, finances, and the land's soil and water.

Environmental Data

Beginning in September 1998, TFRP staff returned monthly to update survey data and collect information about ongoing consumption and environmental conditions. Soil and water measurements were a particularly useful quality-of-life gauge, especially among the many farmers surveyed. After a property owner had completed a monthly soil questionnaire, a specially trained enumerator took a closer look at the respondent's land on his own.

Using a handheld global positioning system, the environmental enumerator visited a specific plot, and took samples from the top 20 centimeters of soil with a T-handled probe. Slivers of dirt from five spots, along a W-shaped transect spanning the plot, would be analyzed later for soil fertility indicators such as nitrogen levels, pH, organic matter content, and field capacity. The same method was used with a device that measured soil moisture tension and temperature. The tester photographed the plot diagonally across and then again from its center looking north, south, east, and west. To complete the environmental perspective, the tester took notes on the surrounding landscape's vegetation, topography, proximity to water bodies, and other salient details.

Because soil is worthless without water, the tester was also responsible for charting rainfall amounts via gauges in each target village, and, for the survey's first year, groundwater conditions. Twice weekly, and after the first rain of each month, the tester visited five designated groundwater sites per village, including canals, streams, ponds, and the occasional well or rainwater cistern, measuring the water's pH, temperature, and conductivity. A monthly lab test looked at concentrations of chemicals such as nitrogen and phosphorus in the water.

Box 4.1
Rainfall in Thailand

> The survey sites in the Townsend Thai Project note differences in agricultural production, due in large part to regional differences in topography. One of the metrics used in the survey documents rainfall variances in rural areas. During the last few decades, Bangkok has suffered land subsidence caused by lowering water tables due to over reliance on the Chao Phraya River. Warm, rainy monsoons converge from mid-May to September. The dry, cool monsoons appear from November to mid-March. Thailand's tropical climate has allowed a robust agricultural output, with rice being the principal export crop.

With such valuable information, the researchers were able to examine economic concepts like never before. The combination of socioeconomic survey information and environmental conditions only widened their understanding.

One area of understanding that grew was in the measurement of productivity. Good growing conditions required a delicate combination of the amount of rainfall and soil quality. Without environmental data on soil quality and rainfall, researchers could not study the increased productivity of fertilizer application, since they had no comparison point or knowledge of what the unfertilized soil would have yielded. Also, by knowing these environmental factors about a farmer's plot, researchers could use them as a control to determine if two fields yielded the same amount of crop because of higher fertilizer application to one field, which had lower quality soil, or because the farmer managed the other field less efficiently.

But the benefits of the data did not end there. What if a farmer wanted to purchase fertilizer before his or her harvest? The farmer would have to borrow the money to purchase the fertilizer from a formal financial institution (like a bank) or borrow it through informal social networks (like family or other villagers). Researchers identified this trend and were able to determine which groups of farmers were most vulnerable: those with inferior land and few social relations they could rely on.

Length and Localization

While the unique opportunities for research presented by the monthly data were abundant, the survey work was demanding at first, not only for the enumerators getting accustomed to the job but also for the families they visited. Although the questionnaire's time focus was relatively short—only a month's worth of expenditures, savings, and crop harvest—the detail required was profuse. The survey's 22 sections, or modules, were filled with lengthy questions and sub-questions that covered everything from the grading system in a child's school to the brand of fertilizer a farmer preferred. In all, there were almost 3,000 variables and subvariables. The length of the survey, along with the additional time it took to create a roster for households to be interviewed, began to dissuade households from cooperating.

Recognizing the inconvenience, TFRP decided to break up the monthly survey into module groups. This way, by grouping the forms and topics to be covered, more frequent, shorter interviews could be made, ensuring attention span and decreasing boredom. This allowed the monthly interviews to take no longer than 1.5 hours at a time. The survey team came back 3 or 4 times per month, within the time frame of 30 to 40 days of initiated contact, to complete the extensive survey. Because the households were also working, the survey team made themselves available 24/7 so that households could work the interviews into their leisure time.

Even with the efforts to streamline the process, the survey took a considerable amount of work. New enumerators felt they had won a battle if they managed to accurately collect all the necessary monthly information over the course of three or four interviews with one household. Each enumerator was expected to canvas 18 to 20 households over 45 days, for a total of 72 to 100 interviews.

Furthermore, enumerators had to remember that some modules were only applicable in certain places. For example, questions about fishing were key among Chachoengsao's many shrimp and catfish farms but irrelevant amid the cassava fields of Buriram. Some modules would need special attention in certain areas. One example is the land cultivation module, which was an especially important set of questions in Lop Buri, where ideal weather and soil conditions allow farmers to rotate crops frequently. Conversely, the module regarding hired labor could be largely overlooked in Lop Buri, but it was a significant part of many interviews done in Sisaket and Buriram.

Certain modules, such as one about cultivation, caused problems for enumerators in every province because of the high level of detail and specificity required in describing the various, often complex, phases of farming. In the case of a module concerning hired labor, the enumerators' confusion led to a change in the instrument. The section was expanded so that enumerators had codes to record the unexpectedly diverse methods of hiring (such as using labor brokers) and payment (such as crops or food) practiced by some farmers.

During the interviews, enumerators struggled to make complex questions understandable. They found themselves simplifying formal language and economic terms that cropped up. They softened the tone of some questions to make them less direct and more polite, to conform to Thai cultural standards. Instead of saying, "Tell me about your assets," an enumerator might evoke a better response by prompting the interviewee with, "So, what kind of machines do you have for rice farming?"

Adding to the complication, enumerators were sometimes faced with households too reticent to share certain financial information. Enumerators sometimes changed interviewees, looking elsewhere for data. In the rare instances where nervous households persisted in with-holding information, despite visits by field editors and even by Khun Sombat, TFRP recruited new households.

Guides Standardize, Conversations Clarify

Foreseeing some of the confusion, Khun Sombat had compiled thick manuals for enumerators. The instructions covered everything from measuring rainfall accurately to explaining the survey data's confiden-tiality. Enumerators turned to the guide frequently. Is it a good idea to give out a personal phone number? (Yes, it helps build trust.) What's the best way to break up an interview over several sessions? (Cover a certain number of agreed-upon modules during each session.) What should you say if one household inquires about the financial data of another? (Answer indirectly, saying something like, "I haven't asked them about that yet.")

An effort was also made to be conscientious of a household's time. In the case of one extremely busy egg farm operator in Chachoengsao, the enumerator sometimes deferred to farm workers for the remaining information. Because the chicken farm was a large business, the owner and household members hired a large number of workers to raise the chickens, which included feeding, cleaning, egg collecting, and egg selecting. The household members only focused on exporting the eggs to the market, collecting money, and communicating with the bank and feed suppliers. When it came time for the enumerator to question the household, it was clear that the owner could only provide information on the business end and could not provide adequate information on the chicken-raising process. The enumerator allowed the workers responsible for those parts of the process to inform the survey instead, and their answers were subsequently accepted and approved by the household.

With these solutions and others, the monthly surveys gained momen-tum, and the project encountered fewer problems as enumerators gained more experience, became more comfortable, and learned from their co-workers. At monthly planning meetings and occasional infor-mal gatherings at noodle shops, field editors and enumerators would discuss common mistakes, clarify the intent of certain questions, and point out how to approach complex details—what to be aware of and how to handle them more efficiently.

Training and Planning

 TFRP also paid careful attention to planning before the execution of surveys and resurveys, in part by creating a Project Planning Matrix (or "PPM"). This document covered the overarching processes of the monthly, annual rural, and annual urban resurvey, including an extensive operational plan consisting of dates of activities, activity details, the persons responsible for each activity, the tools/materials required for each activity, and the budget for each. When the survey required support from additional staff, the PPM allowed for faster personnel management and provided an easily accessible overview of the survey's interrelated workings. On a more focused level, TFRP enacted a monthly plan of operation geared precisely to the monthly survey. This planning matrix featured each interviewee's scheduled time to meet with the enumerator, dates on which data was entered and verified, data correction done by the field editor and assistant, and included as well the schedule for the field editor and assistant's meetings with the households.

Informal gatherings were not the only source of learning for enumerators. A few times a year, field editors from the four target provinces would meet at TFRP's central office to discuss error patterns and share ideas. These meetings included guest speakers on various topics such as enhancing team work, creating an operational plan, and working with communities (e.g., understanding different religions, traditions, and cultures). Enumerators also learned to be careful in verifying data and to question their own preconceptions. To illustrate the point, Khun Sombat told a story of how, during a field survey practice, he had listened to an enumerator ask a poor, elderly Hmong man whether he owned a refrigerator. The man, not fully understanding, as there was no such word in his dialect, motioned to an old refrigerator in the corner of his humble house. As it turned out, there was no electricity in the village. The man had been using the appliance as a cupboard.

As time went on, enumerators were better able to explain their surveys through simple language and examples. They grew more adept at picking up on clues in the interviewees' behavior and sensing half-truths in rushed answers, for example. They noticed things that may have gone unmentioned, such as a newly purchased piece of farm equipment in the field or a shiny motorbike parked under the house, and used that information to better probe the answers that interviewees offered and ensure the thorough recording of information. They were careful to check names against household rosters and verify details through records such as shopping lists and receipts. To keep the interview from bogging down, and possibly losing the interviewee's interest, some enumerators became familiar enough with the questionnaire that they could jot down short-hand answers to be entered later, rather than finding and entering the proper codes while the household members waited.

To reduce the burden of remembering a whole month's worth of spending, households were asked biweekly to estimate how much they had spent on regular purchases, like food. Interviewees, with repetition and growing accustomed to the process, began to anticipate questions with ready answers, writing them out beforehand in some cases. Interviews went from four-hour ordeals to one- or two-hour conversations.

Building Trust

Completion was one thing. Trust was another.

It was easy for enumerators to tell households that their information would be kept confidential and their participation furthered a good cause. It was more difficult to convince them. As with any relationship, it took time for the two sides to understand each other. The foundation for this understanding, in most cases, was built on courtesy, consideration, and compassion.

Enumerators were careful always to be deferential and to inquire about a household's well-being any time they met. To steer small talk, they might try to discern the interviewee's interests by commenting on artwork or other objects in the house. They visited household family members in the hospital and, using a 3,200-baht monthly office fund, gave gifts such as fish sauce, drinking glasses, or blankets for New Year's, at monks' ordination ceremonies, and to celebrate births. For funerals, they gave a 200-baht (about 6 USD) wreath and offered 300 baht (about 9 USD) for service costs. Enumerators were encouraged not to just send gifts for, but also to attend, funerals and marriages. Many elderly interviewees enjoyed their time with enumerators as a respite from loneliness, and some poor households saw their participation as a way of making a nonfinancial donation to worthy research.

While many people in the United States feel comfortable expressing strong opinions or proffering advice about a topic in casual conversation, in Thai culture it's less acceptable to voice an opinion in a manner that suggests the listener should follow the speaker's advice. TFRP sees giving suggestions as beyond its scope and policy, but sharing opinions about the usage of chemical fertilizers and pesticides—for example among TFRP enumerators and interviewees who share an agricultural background—is not uncommon. Sometimes households seek guidance from enumerators who may have more years of formal education. For instance, when one household member quit his job working at a factory, he became overwhelmed by the complexity of the income taxation form he was asked to fill out. The enumerator for that household walked him through the questions the form asked, as the household member filled in his own responses. Other rural households without vehicles might ask an enumerator to run an errand for them in the city or bring an elder to the hospital on the way of their commute.

While TFRP never advocates providing services to the households, small assistance is permissible and furthers strong relationships with the household members and communities. In all of its years of operation, TFRP has enjoyed the trust and cooperation of the villages it operates within; TFRP is careful to support the communities by spending nights locally and purchasing food and necessities within the community during their stay. Only rarely will a team stay in a hotel.

These relationships, however, were not always easily won. On a few occasions, enumerators showed up for interviews to find curious people loitering. In one such interview, at a household member's shop in Chachoengsao, strangers peppered an enumerator with accusatory questions and innuendoes about the survey's purpose. Uncomfortable and resentful of being cornered, the enumerator nonetheless approached the situation as a diplomatic opportunity. She politely and thoroughly answered every question, doing her best to dispel suspicions that survey participation would lead to higher taxes.

Of course, enumerators learned that sometimes it was better to say nothing at all. A wife confided details of her husband's adultery, resulting in an additional two to three hours that enumerators spent at the household, as the couple argued. During an interview in Lop Buri, a household dispute over a motorbike ended when a young man struck his father in the head with the back of a hatchet. One mentally unstable interviewee was known to walk around with a machete, asking people whether they thought it was sharp enough. A shop owner repeatedly insisted that he would not discuss his finances.

In these cases, enumerators listened politely without responding prematurely, and then redirected questions, rescheduled interviews, or asked their field editors to replace the household within the survey. For instance, in the case of the son attacking this father, it became clear that a substance addiction was involved. To uphold the integrity of the survey, TFRP ended the household's participation in it and found a substitute.

A more humorous anecdote concerns an old man who sat for an interview in his adult son's house. The man rattled off answers to the enumerator's questions for more than an hour before he realized something was wrong. He had been describing his son's finances instead of his own. The interview began again.

In some cases, TFRP had to deal with enumerators who stepped out of bounds. One such incident involved a young man in Sisaket who often brought a bottle of whiskey to drink with a particular target household. The enumerator was given a stern warning. When his behavior persisted, the young man was asked to leave. Subsequently, the household was no longer willing to be interviewed and was also replaced. After that incident, TFRP made the decision to institute a policy that enumerators were not able to drink publicly in their survey communities in order to maintain credibility in more conservative areas.

Like mailmen on their routes, enumerators occasionally had to beware of dogs at certain homes. For a time, rowdy teenagers in one Buriram village had female enumerators nervous about making their rounds. Night-time frog hunters pulled up soil moisture devices used by the environmental enumerators, taking sensitive wiring to use in their flashlights. A few target households moved away suddenly for work in other provinces, saying they would return, but never did so. One woman, exhausted from raising several children and running a store, fell asleep during evening interviews.

Staff conflicts were not unheard of either. Morale plummeted in Sisaket when the field editor there insisted on working separately from the enumerators and carried on relations with her boyfriend in plain view of the office. One soil analyst found himself without time or energy to do his job after his girlfriend left him and their three-year-old son.

Clearly, there was no shortage of obstacles in those first few years of the monthly survey. Solutions came by way of diplomacy, community awareness, careful and detail-oriented work, adaptation, firm standards, and common sense.

As for the frog hunters, Khun Sombat simply spread the word through local leaders and others that the soil gauges were essential to the project and could eventually provide invaluable information for the community. Frog hunters heeded the message.

Of course, since the survey is an ongoing process with human beings, some problems with the survey staff were unavoidable and required protocol. For instance, staff members were discharged when problems were big or violations were repeated. If a behavioral issue should arise, the data from their past interviews were checked; TFRP institutionalized a cross-check system, with random re-interviews of up to 10 to 15 percent of the sample on a regular, consistent basis for the monthly surveys.

TFRP also had strict rules on topics to avoid. Particularly, the staff was instructed to not discuss or get involved in political activities, both at regional and national levels, so as to maintain unbiased data. The staff was also instructed to avoid presenting the data to other persons or organizations.

Sometimes conflicts required individual or creatively unique solutions. It was understandable to ask a household to hold back their dog or to replace an interviewee too tired to answer questions. Less obvious was the way Khun Sombat disarmed the unruly Buriram teens. Instead of confronting them, he introduced himself, chatted, and even sang bawdy songs with the boys. Soon, Khun Sombat had won their respect and an unspoken promise to respect the enumerators.

Helping the soil tester get back on his feet was a matter of hiring a local couple familiar with the work to fill in temporarily. Dealing with the amorous field editor in Sisaket was more complicated, involving a thorough discussion—with both sides of the story—at TFRP's central office. Khun Sombat ultimately decided to discipline and reassign the field editor.

Reassigning households, however, was yet another problem to be solved. When target households moved away, TFRP should take risk-balancing measures, advised Anna Paulson, who had also answered staff questions during the resurvey. To be safe, she wrote in one of many emails, teams should replace families that claimed to be leaving temporarily in case they never returned. Otherwise the survey might shrink to the point of obsolescence.

From the beginning, TFRP has used the common survey research method of random sampling. Therefore, when TFRP selected households to interview for the baseline data, a list was also then compiled of back-up households, in case any of the households chosen for interviewing exited. Generally, a household would exit if the family moved away. Rarely would a household refuse to continue interviewing. If so, the field supervisor and field editor would make a trip to the household in order to hear their concerns and provide additional information about the purpose of the survey. After that meeting, most households changed their minds and continued to cooperate with the survey team, leaving only a small fraction of households voluntarily leaving the survey each year. Replacing these households who leave is a key to the integrity of the survey.

Profile: Boom

Managing the monthly survey, the most frequent and most detailed of TFRP surveys, requires strict adherence to established systems and policies mixed with innovation and a strong sense of fairness. Punnida "Boom" Thanapoltaverat, the monthly surveys' head supervisor, is the walking embodiment of those characteristics. She has overseen the monthly survey since 2003, having worked as a field editor in Buriram for two years and Lop Buri for four.

Boom's petite size and normally quiet demeanor belie her forceful personality and strong opinions often delivered in staccato bursts. Despite having lost her arm to a childhood accident and suffering discrimination in the form of job rejections as a result, Boom is uninterested in pity and rarely offers it to others. Excuses are often just that, she says, and no field editor or enumerator gets off easy under her watch.

When she was a girl, Boom wanted to be a teacher. She was inspired by one particular instructor who gave equal attention to every student instead of only the smartest pupils, as often happens in Thai primary schools.

Her interest in equal opportunity issues led Boom to family law. The top student in her class at Thammasat University law school, she graduated in three years. Despite her academic success, Boom found many doors closed to her because of her disability. An old professor mentioned TFRP—then in its infancy—and the promise it held for social justice. Boom applied and never looked back.

In Buriram, she found an office with few rules and a staff that moved at an almost lackadaisical pace. She instituted mandatory schedules for interviews and data entry. To cut down on sloppy, rushed work, enumerators were limited to two interviews a day. When enumerators complained, Boom held a meeting and asked them to argue their case as a lawyer might by listing advantages of the old system. No one could present a winning argument.

While her changes did not go over well at first, enumerators came to see their wisdom. The rules made time management easier and data more dependable. Like her staff, Boom was still in her early 20s.

Not wanting to be seen as a task master, Boom would spend hours during and after work chatting with enumerators, making them feel comfortable. Boom's experiments in tweaking procedure carried over—if not always so smoothly—to her time in Lop Buri. Upon taking her post there, she discovered an office as disorganized as Buriram's had been initially. One enumerator had neglected to submit any work for several months. Boom informed the man his salary would be withheld until he could produce the backlogged work. In a rage, the man's wife, who happened to be the office's assistant field editor, came to Boom waving a kitchen knife and banging a table. Boom calmed the woman, telling her it was nothing personal.

The enumerator and his wife left TFRP shortly thereafter. Boom pointed to the experience as ample justification for new rules concerning work schedules. Salaries would be delayed by one week for each day an enumerator was late in completing or turning in a survey. But, Boom made clear, she would be reasonable, considering all factors and listening to enumerators' explanations.

Boom would also advocate on enumerators' behalf with survey respondents. In one such instance, she intervened with a household that wanted to quit the survey rather than risk their financial information falling into the hands of a family they had been feuding with. Boom convinced them of the project's confidentiality and the value of their participation.

As a supervisor Boom maintained her reputation for strictness balanced with openness. While she is quick to show disappointment in anyone sidestepping protocol or doing a lackluster job, Boom is just as fast to encourage field editors to call her with problems at any hour of any day—and they do. If a staff problem does not affect the quality of work, Boom entrusts team members to work out the issues among themselves.

Boom and Khun Sombat encourage enumerators and field editors to take second jobs or at least consider backup work. Some help run their families' farms or work in shops, while others study for advanced degrees. The survey will not last forever, they know, and the pay is modest.

Monthly survey staff members consistently repay Boom with diligence and attention to detail. Field editors, for example, are required to create data entry queries every month. The queries, based on local conditions such as harvest times and household compositions, help check for human error when enumerators enter survey data into a computer system. Field editors consistently create more than the monthly requirement of ten queries. This is tribute, indeed, considering many TFRP staff work one and sometimes two other jobs.

While its goals may be academic, TFRP operates like a lean business. Managing his budget effectively and frugally has become somewhat of an art for Khun Sombat and his staff. Research grant funding from Townsend for the monthly survey, for example, came to about 20,000 USD per month initially. Khun Sombat consistently managed to spend less than the allotted amount, leaving a small reserve for new computers and office furniture.

Khun Sombat's sister-in-law, an accountant, initially helped handle the books for a nominal fee, while Khun Sombat translated surveys into Thai to avoid having to hire costly translators. Khun Sombat's daughter and son-in-law oversee all data cleaning (i.e., the process in which the data is checked and readied for entering into a researchable database), while earning lower-than-normal salaries. For TFRP's first eight years, the operation ran on mostly secondhand and rebuilt computers.

Instead of having a printing house produce the thousands of survey answer forms needed every month, TFRP has for years relied on a single Kyocera printer at the central office. The machine long ago surpassed the manufacturer's claimed lifetime capacity of 1 million copies and has since eclipsed 10 million. Having heard of the printer's exploits, Kyocera provides free maintenance. A photograph of the printer hangs on a wall at the company's Japan headquarters.

Personnel and Compensation

Because staff salaries account for 75 percent of TFRP's funds, Khun Sombat has been careful to streamline employee roles. After the second year of the monthly survey, Khun Sombat asked field editors to trim their staffs of anyone who had worked below potential, consistently made excessive mistakes, or, in a few rare instances, cut corners with data. Additionally, by training enumerators in data entry, field editors eliminated the need for a designated keypunch operator. Field offices went from staffs of 12 or 13 members each to 8 or 9.

While the cutbacks increased enumerators' workloads more than 30 percent, from 15 households to 20, they were given an extra 15 days, or 50 percent more time, to complete the work. Instead of earning a salary as before, they were paid for production. Each completed resurvey interview netted 285 baht (about 8.50 USD). Because most staff drove motorbikes on their rounds, they received monthly gas reimbursements of 250 to 300 baht (about 7.50 to 9.00 USD).

The initiative-based pay plan, combined with schedule flexibility that allowed staff to work second jobs, made attrition rare. On average, only one or two employees leave TFRP each year to take teaching, central government, or local administration jobs.

At first, Khun Sombat paid into health and life insurance plans for his staff. In 2001, three years into the resurvey plan, then-prime minister Thaksin Shinawatra introduced a 30-Baht Scheme (about 1.00 USD) universal insurance plan, and Khun Sombat asked employees to switch, thereby saving TFRP a significant amount of money.

Some financial management changes have been unrelated to cutting costs. To help employees manage their money and prepare for the future, Khun Sombat set up a staff savings and credit fund in the second year of the monthly survey. Three percent of monthly salaries, plus an equal amount from the general fund, goes into the fund. Employees can apply to an elected staff panel for low-interest loans from the fund, which now totals more than 1 million baht (about 30,000 USD).

Box 4.2
30-Baht Scheme

One of the programs in 2001, the universal healthcare program known as the 30-Baht Scheme, has seen tremendous popularity as an outlay for health services. This form of healthcare, which required a minimal co-payment for health services (30 baht is equivalent to 0.90 USD), surged in use especially among lower-income Thais. The basis for the program is to merge and expand upon the Civil Servant Medical Benefit Scheme, the Social Security Scheme, and the Workmen Compensation Fund.

Khun Sombat has made loans to TFRP itself over the years. On two occasions, when processing snafus held up badly needed grant funding, Khun Sombat temporarily bailed out the project with a total of 700,000 baht (about 21,000 USD). Khun Sombat does not pay himself for the frequent overtime he puts in.

How much longer will Khun Sombat, now in his 60s, drive the bumpy back roads to the far-flung villages at the heart of TFRP's monthly survey? "Who knows," he says. He's interested and engaged as long as there are interesting revelations to be made. He mentions occasional discoveries, such as grand houses that hide massive debt and humble farmsteads that sit on tremendous wealth.

Whether it's enhancing the quality of data through more thorough checks or encouraging more inter-staff communication through frequent supervisor visits to field offices, Khun Sombat has been a conscientious leader. The survey's scope can and should be extended, he believes. He's working to add more questions about health and education, among other topics.

There's always room to improve, Khun Sombat says.

5 Developing the Information Systems: Local Knowledge and Global Technologies

The monkhood didn't exactly suit him.

In 1999, Pavisanat "Eu" Pathomcharoensukchai was fresh out of college with a computer engineering degree in his hand and visions of entrepreneurial greatness in his head. He foresaw a future running a multinational computer manufacturing corporation. Silent meditation and deep introspection were not high on the 21-year-old's list of priorities.

But, Eu's ambitions would have to be put on hold. His parents made it clear that they expected their eldest son to initially work at the family pet food factory. If he had to defer his plans, Eu figured he would take the opportunity to become a novice monk. Like many Thai males his age, Eu was expected to steep himself in Buddhist practice, however briefly. While few wear the turmeric-colored robes for life, any length of holy service is considered an honor and source of great merit for one's family.

Eu began as all candidates for the monkhood do in Thailand: by praying to his ancestors. Then, he bathed the feet of his parents and grandparents, who, in turn, cut Eu's shiny hair until only a few patches remained. A monk from the local temple stepped in to shave Eu's eyebrows. The family elders rinsed Eu with bowls of water and blessings over his head. A yellowish herbal rub completed the job, readying Eu to progress with his family to the temple. There, he was surrounded by a *sangha* or "community" of monks. Eu sat prostrated, listening to sermons on Buddhist tenets, vowing to follow the precepts, including a prohibition on dancing, singing, making music, drinking alcohol, and the killing of living beings. Then the young man wore the robes for the first time.

The days that followed quickly blurred into each other for Eu. He woke up at four a.m. every day, bathed, and wrapped himself in his robe—a complex process that might take a novice 30 or 40 minutes.

Box 5.1
The Religious Economy in Thailand

By entering the monkhood, a Thai male increases the merit of his family. In Thai culture, making merit is done with the hope of gaining health, wealth, and happiness. The idea of merit is closely tied to the idea of karma, a gauge of existence of sorts. One's karma is dependent upon the level of merit (or demerit) at any given time and is believed to affect the outcomes of both this life and the next.

Merit can also increase when a Thai family makes a donation to one of the Buddhist temples. This act usually coincides with a ceremony, either in honor of the donation, in thanksgiving, or commonly during robe-giving ceremonies. However, the temple is the not only entity that benefits. Many local economies make substantial profits from ceremonial almsgiving, including local food vendors (from whom the family may purchase food for the monks) as well as artisans who craft gifts. A family may also visit a local market where items used by monks are sold. Donations are diverse and can include land and even furniture.

Another aspect of the religious economy of Thailand is the making and selling of amulets. An individual might chose to rent an amulet, a Buddhist pendant that can be worn or displayed and is thought to ward off misfortune, promote good health, and even increase wealth. The value of an amulet is correlated with the monk who has prayed and chanted with the amulet. Some collectors will pay large fees for amulets, which were used or made by renowned deceased monks.

Then, for two hours, Eu and the other monks walked barefoot over red stone roads begging silently for alms. Simple meals for breakfast, cleaning duties, and multiple prayer sessions rounded out his existence.

For Eu, the greatest hardship was his separation from Tippatavee "Oop," Khun Sombat's daughter. The two had met in elementary school and had become friends in high school. Romance followed.

While Oop visited Eu at the temple several times a week, intimacy was impossible. The two would sit on a bench under a giant tree, sharing lunch and chatting. Oop, 20 years old and in her final year at Suan Dusit Rajabhat University, often peppered Eu with questions about her computer science coursework. She also asked her boyfriend for advice on designing a data checking program for TFRP, an initiative she was helping her father with part-time. She left stacks of programming code pages and two weighty guides to Visual Basic, user-friendly software that Oop wanted to introduce to TFRP. Maybe Eu could help her add more functions to the TFRP program she was working on.

With little to do in his spare time, Eu read the programming books and taught himself the computer language Visual Basic. Lacking a computer at the temple, Eu spent four or five hours every day for a month and a half handwriting codes for data entry and checking commands. Oop would run the codes on her computer and report back the results.

Almost two months after entering the temple confines, Eu left.

When TFRP first launched in the late 1990s, some enumerators had never seen a computer before. Money, staff, infrastructure, and technology were limited. Field offices set up after the baseline survey were each equipped with two second-hand computers that ran on slow Pentium I chips. There were no phone lines in the field, let alone Internet connections. Compiled data from the monthly and annual surveys came to TFRP's central office on floppy discs delivered by hand. It was not uncommon for a disk to arrive damaged or unreadable.

The overall data system went something like this: question, answer, coding, checking, data entry, more checking, then cleaning or readying for research. Table 5.1 shows the job descriptions and number of employees filling those roles in TFRP's data processing team.

Table 5.1
Data Processing Staff at TFRP as of 2011

The **data storage and processing manager** oversees all of the data for public release, working closely with the US-based data manager and other members of the research team to ensure data quality and preservation. He remains the key contact for researchers when data anomalies arise or if questions need to be revised or added to the surveys. Finally, the data storage and processing manager works closely with UTCC to consult on data storage and the preservation of both primary and secondary data.

The **data cleaning manager** oversees all the data cleaning tasks for the annual and monthly surveys. She monitors the data entry, cleaning, and translation and performs advanced query checks to ensure data consistency. The data cleaning manager oversees data checking activities to maintain data quality, works with all field offices, coordinates activities, and manages staff.

Three people make up the **data cleaning staff**. The staff's responsibility is to conduct module checking, address any issues in translation, create and label the data and meta-data, and complete cross-tab checking, data cleaning, and documentation.

Six people make up the **data processing staff**. The staff remains responsible for data transmission control, importing data to the server, keypunching data into the database management system (in the second round), and comparing both rounds of data to find inconsistencies.

The project employs four **keypunch operators**. They enter data from the written questionnaires into TFRP's database software during the first round of keying in data.

Enumerators conducted survey interviews and then translated responses into corresponding codes, using codebooks. For example, 1 signified "yes," while 3 meant "no" in the monthly survey; 97 was the code for "inapplicable," and 98 equated with "does not know the answer." Thorough research and questionnaire pre-testing had created a formidable dictionary of codes for enumerators to choose from. Still, unanticipated answers crept up occasionally, often leading to the creation of yet more codes.

Field editors and team supervisors then read over the completed answer booklets, checking the original long-form responses and their coded equivalents. A field editor might call a bank to check a loan rate quoted by a household or pay a random visit to review information with an interviewee. Baseline data, such as annual income and expenditures or previous months' responses, aided the financial sleuth work.

TFRP also took advantage of a set of questions in the annual resurvey called the Risk and Response Module. During this part of the survey, enumerators engaged in more informal conversation about the well-being of the household (family, children, occupation, etc.) during the last 12 months, keeping with Thai culture to politely ask about such subjects when seeing someone again. Certain responses alerted enumerators to keep events on their radar throughout the subsequent survey. For instance, if a family member mentioned that another member had fallen ill, enumerators realized this might have affected the household's expenses, savings, or borrowing. During those sections of the survey, an enumerator would jog the family member's memory by saying, "You mentioned your sister was ill. How did you cover her hospital expenses?"

The ethnographic mapping tools also proved to be of great importance when creating consistency in responses. Because TFRP mapped and recorded the agricultural details of the village (who planted which crops and so on), along with occupational information, the enumerators entered the interview with an idea of what to expect each household's situation to be. Satellite photo technology, brought to the project by Michael Binford, was used to track the number of *rai* (a measurement of acreage) used by households.

The task of ensuring accurate responses was one thing. Catching errors through coding and data entry proved to be another. Initially, the nonprofit research group RAND (Research and Development) Corporation was brought in as a consultant for data systems. Data entry and English translation work were subcontracted to the well-known

Chulalongkorn University in Bangkok. There, specially trained students working on 20 computers in the nursing school—there was no space available elsewhere—put the information through several hurdles. First, the Chulalongkorn students entered in a database codes corresponding to the long-form answers submitted. These coded answers were then matched up against the coded answers supplied by field offices. Discrepancies were flagged and brought to supervisors' attention. This "double blind" system ensured information on the questionnaires was not blurred by keypunch errors. This system, installed at the beginning of the project for the Big Survey, was critical to TFRP's success in producing thoroughly vetted data.

The computer program TFRP used in the beginning, however, was problematic. The ISSA-LAN platform (the abbreviations stand for "integrated system for structural analysis" and "local area network," terms that barely hint at the complications involved) that RAND utilized was less than ideal. The DOS-based program (Disk Operating System) ran slowly and had a confusing data storage system, involving dozens of separate folders. To deal with the questionnaire's separate modules, it was necessary to operate separate ISSA-LAN-based programs on separate computers. It took an hour and a half to enter coded data from one relatively simple resurvey answer sheet. The outdated ISSA database would continue to cause problems for the first three years of the annual resurvey.

Like any raw product, the Townsend Thai Data were designed to be processed. The processing factory, in this case, was the National Opinion Research Center (NORC) in Chicago, where data were "cleaned" or checked to ensure that the answers entered in the database corresponded to their designated codes. From there, data were made ready for use by researchers in a searchable database. As with the process still carried out today, unanswered questions were tabulated, with overall response rates reflecting that some questions were not applicable (e.g., asking about the education of children when, in fact, a household had no children). Tables of mean, standard deviation, and minimum-maximum figures for each variable were created. Programmers ran data through software to convert them into a usable format and then assigned definitions and error codes to variables. Along the way, data cleaners amassed a "dictionary" of coding errors and solutions.

It soon became clear, however, that something had been lost in translation, literally and figuratively. The translations from Chulalongkorn were not as good as had been hoped for. There were problems translating answers—often given in local dialects—into English. Certain rural cultural data caused confusion among the city-dwelling programmers. On top of this, Khun Sombat and Townsend were left with only a few computers after the first year. As had been RAND's standard practice, they donated TFRP's equipment to Chulalongkorn, assuming the survey would last only that one round.

Khun Sombat took what was useful from the RAND consultant's advice and began thinking about how to create a better system. Khun Sombat moved all his operations and remaining equipment from Chulalongkorn to his Bangkok office and brought in various information technology experts. Ultimately, in 1999, he hired a team of Rajabhat University students with computer science backgrounds.

Led by Oop, Khun Sombat's daughter, the team of seven was charged to create a more accurate, user-friendly, efficient, and flexible data processing program. The pay was little, and the hours—evenings after classes and during weekends and holidays—were less than ideal. But the significance of what they were doing was not lost on them, either. Few of their classmates could say they were working on a data-sorting program for a groundbreaking research project of international importance.

Redesigning the DOS-based ISSA-LAN program was out of the question. It lacked the flexibility to handle even the straightforward annual survey efficiently. Tweaking it to process the massive and complex amount of monthly survey data would be next to impossible. Additionally, the only programming manual on hand was in Spanish.

So, the redesign team set two basic but ambitious goals for itself: map and understand the ISSA-LAN program, then replace it.

Toward that end, Oop and the others on the team spent months trying to find where the ISSA-LAN program stored data. After discovering the program's data format, programmers went about extracting and converting it into text files. From there, they switched over to the easier-to-use Visual Basic and Microsoft Access platforms.

Six months after they began, the redesign team had a workable program. By 2000, the new system was ready to be implemented. It was faster and could be modified for future survey changes. Survey questions now appeared on the data entry screen, and Thai language answers could be entered directly, leaving subsequent translation to English as a separate issue.

While Oop stayed on to refine the program and train staff to use it, the rest of the team gradually went their separate ways. Most of the team members had graduated from the university by then. Their degrees, combined with their work for TFRP, would garner high-paying software company jobs. What they had done was no small notch on a résumé, but in fact a major achievement. Plus, they had done it without professional outside help.

A month later, Eu joined his girlfriend Oop on the project. Happy to get away from Bangkok for a while, he visited the study's remote field offices. He watched to see how staff entered data in the system, what tripped them up, and what went smoothly. Eu pored over surveys, looking for clues to how people answered open-ended questions. He sat in on a few household survey interviews.

Eu's field study provided one major insight: the program developed by the information technology team for data cleaning was based primarily on the survey questionnaires. There was little human element. To allow the surveys to reflect some of his observations from the field and provide a more streamlined system, Eu scrambled to read up on the necessary coding language for Microsoft Access.

The new system would also need to address the obstacle of responses in Thai. The issue of integrating language and open-ended answers and producing an English-language dataset required a truly innovative solution. The program needed to work not only with the Thai language but also with its various dialects. It also became clear that asking for translation of all the open-ended responses was unwieldy and time-consuming.

Eu and Oop's solution was innovative. The new program systematically grouped similar Thai responses from each questionnaire and created a translation dictionary, specialized with the modules and variables in mind. Once all grouped terms or phrases could be gleaned from the automatic dictionary-assisted translation, the data were verified and those responses still out of the range of the dictionary were sent to professional translators. Once the translated data were sent back, the team examined the translations to see if more terms could be added to the dictionary for future processing.

This entire process helped to speed along the translation and also allowed the dictionary to be a living document. New terminology, like "DVD player," had to be added in order to keep the processing current and relevant. All of these combined efforts reduced translation costs so that simple translations could be easily made automatically with only the complex translations reserved for experts. Having the translated data more easily coded allowed further double-blind checking of more than just numerical data.

With their enhanced adaptability for processing language into viable codes, the new programs would be able to handle many more variables in survey answers. Additionally, it would speed up the data entry process by automatically verifying whether responses to subquestions logically followed responses to main questions. If checkers corrected an error in one response, the new program would make the appropriate corrections in related subquestions. The program now would also detect various mistakes in data entry. For example, if an enumerator accidentally listed a household member as having moved or died, the program would put up a red flag when the household member was later listed as working. TFRP staff would, in coming years, continue to build such queries to contend with newly discovered human errors, ensuring answers that fell within established ranges and modules related to each other appropriately.

The team also improved storage. Instead of a confusing, inconvenient multitude of folders, data storage would be handled in one central location on a server. The 180-gigabyte server would remain at the heart of TFRP's data processing system for years.

Eu stayed busy for months training staff how to use the new data-checking capabilities. Because the system's data entry programs were put in place with limited field testing, bugs crept up occasionally. Eu again traveled regularly among the field offices, installing updates and making repairs.

Some field offices went a step further toward ensuring accurate data, setting penalties for sloppy work. For example, each Lop Buri enumerator was allowed up to 199 mistakes out of thousands of monthly answer booklet entries. The 200th mistake would incur a 100-baht (about 3 USD) fine, with another baht for each mistake thereafter. In Chachoengsao, each enumerator was allowed up to 20 errors in the data entry phase. Any more mistakes and the enumerator would have to review his work with a teammate for the next month.

In addition to field editors' random visits, Khun Sombat began to stop in on target households occasionally to chat and review survey responses. Worried that staff might be alert to pending office visits, Khun Sombat switched up his schedule to ensure he had a realistic view of enumerators' work.

The incentives for careful, efficient work had dramatic effects. Enumerators' growing familiarity with the survey, the nuances of their jobs, and the households they visited also helped to continuously diminish error rates. Over time, computer upgrades would further speed along the checking and cleaning process.

In 2004, TFRP took another major step toward moving the data processing along, assuming responsibility for data cleaning from NORC. Eu went to Chicago that year for two months to learn about the data cleaning process. Upon returning, he installed cleaning software as well as a system that plotted household data on maps for quick visual comparison.

By early 2006, newlyweds Eu and Oop had launched the data cleaning operation with TFRP in earnest. Since then, TFRP's data cleaning team has processed all the annual surveys and now processes all data within roughly six months of its collection. The more data-rich monthly surveys have proven harder to keep up with. However, the time between data collection and cleaning has steadily grown smaller as TFRP's data processing and cleaning capabilities steadily grow faster. Thanks to the automated program Eu and Oop developed, translation is less of an issue. Computer hardware upgrades and Internet connections—made possible by periodic funding secured by Townsend—allows for easy electronic delivery of data from field offices. TFRP's data entry and analysis are now integral parts of its operation.

He could not have known it at the time, but Eu's contemplative period in the monkhood had been the seed for a complex data process.

6 Dreams and Reality: Expanding the Project

Far from the nervous electricity of Bangkok, there is a place where night and day trade places, where the dark before dawn is a time for industry, the light of noontime for dream-addled sleep. From Thailand's capital, set the compass due south. On a map, Satun is almost 1,000 kilometers (620 miles) from Bangkok. To reach it, one must wind all the way down the trunk of the elephant head–shaped country (see figure 6.1). On the pockmarked highway, it's a day and a half of driving. The journey reveals tropical visions: cathedral-like palm tree alleys lining coconut plantations, karstic cliff faces towering over glistening rice paddies.

Satun

The largely Islamic province of Satun leans against Malaysia, picking up radio and television transmissions from the predominantly Muslim country. Satun reaches far into the Andaman Sea, ultimately extending into 105 islands. The expansive harbors have long been destinations for Asian traders, their goods, and their ideas.

The thermometer generally hovers around 28 degrees Celsius (82°F) but occasionally inches toward 40 degrees Celsius (104°F). Rain comes about 180 days a year, leaving behind 156 millimeters—half a foot—of water for the rich soil. Trees loaded with mangosteens, durians, rambutans, and longans grow easily. But it is the rubber tree, planted in symmetrical rows seemingly everywhere, that gives Satun its air of perpetual daydream.

The sun's intense heat stops up the flow of latex sap, so harvesters must tap their rubber trees in the wee morning hours. Between one a.m. and dawn, plantations are aglow with headlamps. During this window of time, rubber farmers slice incisions into their trees' latex vessels, draining the sap that trickles forth into small buckets. Come

Figure 6.1
Map of Thailand

noon, the fresh latex is bound for market and, eventually, tires or shoe soles. By early afternoon, eyelids grow sodden, shops close, streets go quiet, and sleep descends on Satun.

Once a district of the Malay sultanate Kedah, Satun was partitioned from its cultural origins when Siam claimed it (as well as neighboring districts) in a 1909 treaty with the British. Despite this history, Satun managed a peaceful integration with Thailand in 1933. Most foreign visitors to Satun gravitate toward Koh Tarutao, the largest island in an extensive national maritime park. A malarial prison colony during World War II, Koh Tarutao has since reverted to thick jungle full of rare species, pristine waterfalls, beaches, and coral reefs.

Not far away on the mainland, a large fjord-like lake between two mountains is home to the "water dog" or *mah nam*, a toad-like creature that has a tail and barks like a canine. Locals pay close attention to animal noises, particularly those of the *krarang hua juk* or "red-whiskered bulbul," a songbird with a tall pointed black crest and a red face patch. In highly competitive contests, judges listen for the loudest, quickest, and most sustained songs—*kink-a-joo, kink-a-joo*—among dozens of bulbuls in ornate wooden cages. The birds' keepers urge them on with whistles. To the locals, it's serious business. Prize money can approach a million baht (around 30,000 USD).

Satun can be a sensory overload for first-time visitors. From the Day-Glo-colored fishing boats moored along the coast to the bleating goats that wander narrow village streets, the atmosphere can be other-worldly. For enumerators and field editors from the Bangkok area, coming to Satun was as adventurous as crossing an international border. In one village that TFRP staff survey, announcements from the local *por-nor* (the Thai word for a traditional Islamic madrassa, a semi-nary or school) echo over loudspeakers as old women and cats nap on small porches of ancient wooden houses huddled together. Tethered sea hawks are commonly kept as pets.

Change has come fast in recent years to these tradition-bound communities. Thailand's economic crisis hit rubber prices hard, driving down incomes for many. Shifting consumer tastes deflated demand for cholesterol-heavy fruits, like durian and mangosteen, forcing local farmers to replant their fields with oil-bearing palm trees. Deep-sea fishermen introduced the scourge of *yaa baa* or methamphetamine, the drug of choice for long nights of work on the water. Most foreigners were introduced to the region in 2004, when images of the tsunami that devastated this area were broadcast around the globe. Satun's guardian

Box 6.1
Loss of Human Life Following the 2004 Tsunami

The 2004 tsunami remains the largest natural disaster to strike Thailand, with 5,395 people confirmed dead and another 2,817 people missing. In total, an estimated 58,550 were affected by the tsunami.

spirit of the sea, Pra Samut Thewaa, could do little to stop the surging walls of seawater that, as if in a nightmare, killed more than 200,000 across all of Asia and badly damaged Satun's profitable tourism industry.

Years later, visitors would once again return to the region's beaches and to the tsunami's only visible legacy: blue and white evacuation signs. Satun would recover, and the Townsend Thai Data would tell the story. The longest lasting of the expansion target provinces, Satun, provides a colorful case study of how to—and how not to—take survey work into unfamiliar territory.

It was not the daydream atmosphere that attracted Khun Sombat and Townsend. The two colleagues looked to Satun and nearby Yala for other reasons, when they considered expanding TFRP's survey work in 2002. Yala was the poorest province in Thailand's south, a region as a whole relatively overlooked by previous national economic surveys. The local Muslim communities offered a window into a culture little understood by the largely Buddhist country. Landlocked Yala, with its small farms, low education rate, and fundamentalist brand of Islam, presented a contrast to Satun's more open mixture of international culture and commerce.

Khun Sombat and Townsend had discussed their dream of going south for several years but were limited by tight resources. They considered these provinces again with the encouragement of top BAAC officials. At the invitation of the bank's vice president, an old friend, Khun Sombat had given a speech at BAAC headquarters in 2003. He spoke of the baseline survey's success and of TFRP's tremendous potential. Curiosity rippled through the audience: could TFRP help the bank make up for its lack of data beyond Thailand's central region? This would be valuable to the BAAC. With the help of Aleena Adam, a close friend and frequent TFRP collaborator within the BAAC, there was soon an offer: BAAC would fund the cost to replicate the survey in the far south. For Townsend and Khun Sombat, it was another dream realized. Their dream, however, would coincide with a national night-mare for Thailand.

In early 2003, TFRP began laying the groundwork for its expansion to the south. Adam drafted a letter to the bank's branches in the new target provinces. They were to assist TFRP by recruiting local enumerators and smoothing the way with area authorities. Townsend chose target villages based on information from old government surveys. TFRP would start field work that fall.

Things did not go according to plan. The training process went slower than expected. Long-distance logistics, unusual work schedules among rubber farmers, and language difficulties proved potent obstacles for local staff and the households they did pre-testing with. Some enumerators in the south, hired in part for their knowledge of Malay dialects, initially struggled to understand the survey's Thai wording. Once again, TFRP would rely on the unique talents of its staff members to move forward.

Profile: Supanee

The creases that spread out from Supanee Tanjaro's eyes tell stories. In relatively conservative Satun, where many women shroud themselves in headscarves, Supanee is strong willed and independent minded. She laughs loudly and often during her rounds managing a small rubber plantation, raising four children, and running a general store out of her house.

Locals on motorbikes pull up to the shop throughout the day, exchanging gossip and perusing the shelves for single serving packs of Nescafé and Sunsilk shampoo, bottles of Hong Thong Whiskey, light bulbs, and combs. Supanee has financial wisdom to offer as well. She is a board member of the local Million Baht Village Fund, a government-led small business initiative. She also volunteers with a community savings group and a poverty eradication program.

Supanee's role as a respected community leader, with an extensive economics background, made her an ideal choice to spearhead TFRP's survey work in Satun. In 2003, the rural survey's first year in the south, Supanee worked as an enumerator and team leader. Her house was the designated team meeting place, her maturity and knowledge much sought after by the university-aged enumerators.

Most of Satun's local enumerators are young Muslim women. Like Supanee, several of these women juggle survey work with family

Box 6.2
Thai Million Baht Village Fund

Beginning in 2001, Thailand initiated a tremendous microlending program dubbed the Thai Million Baht Village Fund program. The Thai government appropriated 1 million baht (approximately 30,000 USD) to every village and community, regardless of population size, for rotating microcredit. While the funding came from Bangkok, local communities directed the terms, interest rates, conditions, and individual amounts for the money lent locally by way of committees, who were selected by the community and served under the administration of the Government Savings Bank. With nearly 74,000 villages and 4,500 urban and military communities, this infusion of capital quickly amounted to one of the largest examples of targeted microlending on a global scale. By 2002, 92 percent of communities had established Urban Community Fund Committees. As of 2005, 77.5 billion baht, 98.3 percent of the originally scheduled amount, had been distributed for microlending.

responsibilities and latex harvesting. They understand intimately the peculiar local schedule during the dry season, when the rural survey is held. They, too, work rubber trees in the day's dark early hours and want little to do with financial interviews come noon.

Despite introductions by local BAAC credit officers, the survey raised suspicions among some headmen and interviewees. Why their villages? What exactly would their private financial information be used for? And who was the newcomer, a Buddhist from Bangkok, supervising the survey and shuttling enumerators around? There was too much detail required, some households complained. Who could remember how many kilos of rice they had eaten in the past month?

Yet Muslim households appreciated the consideration enumerators accorded them by avoiding visits during prayer times, as well as avoiding questions about liquor consumption. The burden of interview times decreased with increasing familiarity between the villagers and the enumerators; trust solidified when it became clear data would be kept confidential, and the Buddhist newcomer, Laddawan "Bui" Kamkoh, made friends with her easy-going persona.

Bui became a familiar face in Satun over the years, visiting several times to oversee the rural and urban surveys, sometimes working as both a supervisor and a field editor. When, in October 2005, Supanee assumed the title of field editor for Satun's urban survey, it was only a few months after giving birth to her fourth child, a girl. Motherhood, the shop, and the rubber trees left little time for anything else. Supanee's husband, a police officer who works in the city of Hat Yai, about 100 kilometers (60 miles) away, was able to come home for only a few days every other month to help.

It was not long before Supanee was urging Bui to assist her. In coming years, Supanee would return to a hybrid role, in which she coordinated yearly survey schedules with local leaders and interviewed households.

Vision Meets Violence

From the first days of the project's involvement in the south, there were signs of change to come in the social structure of the region. Nowhere were the indicators more alarming, however, than in Yala. A long-simmering separatist movement among the province's ethnic Malays had become established by the time TFRP began carrying out surveys there in 2003. Sporadic bombings and attacks made the national news.

By the summer of 2004, when Townsend and Khun Sombat visited the region to meet with local officials, the situation was dire, although idyllic life in little villages such as Tambon Rae and Mae Haad, ringed with green mountains and clear lakes that mirrored the sky, made it hard to believe. Soft-spoken locals invited Khun Sombat and Townsend in for familial meals of fried fish and omelets. In contrast, it was also there in Bannang Sata District where a policeman directing traffic was shot to death that summer, six marines died in an attack on their outpost, and an assistant village headman was assassinated on his way to a meeting. The sound of military helicopters echoed frequently in the sky.

Faced with the growing threat, TFRP pulled out of Yala in 2004, having completed only one year, an analog to the baseline survey.

Box 6.3
Unrest in the South

In a domestic context, the south of Thailand has experienced unrest since annexing, in 1902, majority Malay-speaking Muslim provinces from the previous Kingdom of Pattani. The provinces of Narathiwat, Yala, Pattani, and Songkhla are no longer under a state of emergency, following a reprieve at the end of 2010 by Prime Minister Abhisit Vejjajiva; nonetheless, flashes of violence continue from separatist groups.

Hopes of returning diminished as the violence continued. BAAC officials suggested Khun Sombat and Townsend shift their Yala resources north to help evaluate new government credit programs there.

While their intention was not to find a substitute for Yala, Khun Sombat and Townsend agreed they had to expand elsewhere, and the northern part of the country was the one region not represented in the survey. The next stop would be the mountainous region bordering Laos and Burma, an area where the BAAC had managed to collect little data. Townsend and Khun Sombat settled on the provinces of Phrae and Phetchabun. By going north, the close friends were completing a circle they had begun in Chiang Mai more than a decade earlier.

Phrae and Phetchabun

The road to Phrae traverses peaks and valleys thick with bamboo, teak, and papaya trees. Rainbow-colored logging trucks groan up and shudder down the slopes with their loads of the area's famous teak wood. Hill tribesmen, Lisu, with their multicolored costumes, and Akha, with their coin-adorned headdresses, ride in the beds of pickup-truck taxis. In the towns, bicycle rickshaws roll by flat-screen television displays in electronics store windows. Some homes still maintain the tradition of putting out clay water pots for travelers and their horses.

Phrae's timber riches attracted foreign attention in the late 1800s. With King Chulalongkorn's consent, the East Asiatic Company of Denmark and the Bombay Burma Company of Britain for decades cut great swaths of mighty teak trees—some as large as lighthouses. Elephants pushed and oxen pulled the logs to the Yom River where they were floated to the great Chao Phraya River and 555 kilometers (345 miles) downstream to Bangkok and Europe-bound freighters.

Unlike the towering teaks of Phrae, Phetchabun's main cash crop, tobacco, stays close to the ground. Because of its tremendously fertile soil, the area was originally dubbed Phuechapura, which means "plenty of crops." Phetchabun means "plenty of diamonds," someone's idea of an improvement to the old name. While a booming diamond market is not in evidence, wide swaths of deforested farmland give credence to the region's reputation as a breadbasket.

From the start of this expansion of the surveys, the local TFRP staff members in Phetchabun and Phrae were augmented with supervisors, field editors, and enumerators from the central office and various field offices. In Phrae, visiting enumerators stayed in a defunct forestry school. Connections with local officials, as usual, proved invaluable in arranging these accommodations. A friend of Khun Sombat's at the provincial forestry department allowed TFRP staff to stay in the department's old dormitory in exchange for payment of the building's utility bills. This arrangement would last for years.

Establishing trust and strong working relationships between TFRP staff members and the local people would be essential from the start. As they have every year since, TFRP supervisors visited the new target provinces to meet with village headmen, savings group directors, and other local leaders. Bearing a letter from the central office and gifts such as a box of prettily wrapped Fuji apples, the supervisors reviewed the basics of the survey and asked for help in coordinating household interviews.

In the northern provinces, where survey taking began in the fall of 2004, the pool of university graduates TFRP would normally hire from was much smaller. The lack of higher education opportunities in Phrae and Phetchabun drove students to pursue their studies elsewhere. As a result, TFRP largely found itself initially with a small, poorly prepared local staff. The arrangement would prove untenable. Because of consistently low-quality work from the staff, Khun Sombat would phase out some of local enumerators in the northern provinces after 2005.

For other reasons, he would phase out Phetchabun altogether. Dropping the northern province was a matter of basic financial management for TFRP. A newly appointed BAAC president had little interest in the survey work and decided to pull funding after 2005. For that final year, the bank would fund only 75 percent of costs in Satun, Phrae, and Phetchabun, forcing Khun Sombat to make up the remaining 25 percent. He turned to the reserve cash. This was a temporary fix, however, and Khun Sombat knew he would have to cut at least one of the new target provinces. Phetchabun's singularly agricultural economy, in contrast to Phrae's diversity of commerce, made it a logical choice for elimination.

Table 6.1 lists and categorizes the types of surveys TFRP implemented across provinces in various regions and for what periods.

Taking Advantage of Obstacles

Before the year 2004 was out, there would be one more major stumble that threatened the future of TFRP's work.

Table 6.1
Implementation of the Townsend Thai Surveys

Province Name	Region	Type of Survey	Date
Chachoengsao	Central	Baseline	1997
		Rural Annual	1998–present
		Monthly	1999–present
		Urban Annual	2005–present
Lop Buri	Central	Baseline	1997
		Rural Annual	1998–present
		Monthly	1999–present
		Urban Annual	2005–present
Buriram	Northeast	Baseline	1997
		Rural Annual	1998–present
		Monthly	1999–present
		Urban Annual	2005–present
Sisaket	Northeast	Baseline	1997
		Rural Annual	1998–present
		Monthly	1999–present
		Urban Annual	2005. present
Satun	Southern	Rural Annual	2003–present
Yala	Southern	Rural Annual	2003
Phrae	Northern	Rural Annual	2004–present
Phetchabun	Northern	Rural Annual	2004

Townsend had told officials at an inaugural conference for the University of Chicago–UTCC Research Center that objective evaluation of government policy was essential. As an example, he cited his analysis of the Thaksin administration's Million Baht Village Fund program. Townsend insisted on a balanced, objective review. Implemented in 2001, the program had spurred consumption, investment, and a number of key measures. On other dimensions, such as loan repayment, however, the program performed less well.

The next morning, a major Thai newspaper ran an article claiming Townsend had criticized the administration for ineffectual economic policy.[1] The professor, through UTCC, immediately sent the papers a full transcript of his comments to show that they had been mischaracterized. But the damage was done. It was not long before the phone rang in Townsend's Bangkok hotel: the prime minister's office wanted an explanation.

The next day, in a private meeting with the prime minister's chief planner and Khun Sombat, Townsend explained his comments and their context. During the course of the three-hour conversation, the mood gradually lifted as the aide came to appreciate the scope and potential import of the survey work. The prime minister's office would do whatever it could to help Townsend and TFRP in dealings with local administrative officials, the aide said. In the meantime, would Townsend consider giving a presentation to an economic committee of the national parliament?

Less than three days after the headlines, Prime Minister Thaksin praised Townsend's research during a television news interview. Thaksin described TFRP as an important source of data for the country's development and prosperity. Later, Khun Sombat would give a three-hour presentation to a committee of senators, familiarizing the legislators with the study and taking their questions.

Bad publicity had turned into a good opportunity.

7 Forging New Ground: Expanding to Urban Areas

In June 2006, Khun Sombat drove to Buriram, near the Cambodia border, for a veteran enumerator's big day. The 29-year-old bride had been with TFRP almost since its beginning. As with all his longtime staff, Khun Sombat considered her among his friends. He often drove up to eight hours to visit with enumerators and field editors, have dinner together, attend the ceremonies that marked their lives; he would stay in touch after they moved on to new careers.

Khun Sombat made a lengthy toast at the wedding reception in Buriram. Standing before some 300 guests, he recalled how he had watched the bride grow into a woman, how he felt like her big brother. Together, they had come a long way. The survey work and its challenges had been their common bond. Rapt silence from the other guests turned to clapping and more toasts.

Almost a decade after the baseline survey, the Thai Project was still rolling, still innovating, and still expanding. While the Buriram wedding a few months earlier had marked a new beginning in the personal life of Khun Sombat's friend and the survey's long-time enumerator, that fall would mark the start of new professional relationships for TRFP staff—among their colleagues and to the work itself. Enumerators would begin a new annual urban survey. The questionnaire was similar to the rural resurvey but with a focus on life and commerce in cities and big towns. TFRP staff would have to adjust to the new terrain, content, interview techniques, and workload, while still completing their regular monthly rural survey work.

The urban survey was born out of the success of the annual and monthly rural resurveys. It was also born of Townsend and Khun Sombat's awareness that they could not complete an economic picture of Thailand without including its towns and cities.

Looking toward urban Thailand, Townsend had inquired about coordinating TFRP rural household survey work with World Bank surveys of large, city-based firms. The idea, however, had sputtered in the face of logistical and budgetary complications. Then, in 2004, Townsend was asked to give a seminar at the Ministry of Finance in Thailand. The invitation came at the urging of ministry staff who had been students of Townsend's during one of his visiting professorships at MIT and from former National Economic and Social Development Board (NESDB) officials who had met Townsend and Khun Sombat during their early visits to government agencies.

Shortly after Townsend's seminar, Ministry of Finance officials approached him with a proposal. Could TFRP collect similar data in urban areas? Ministry officials wanted information on the relationship between household finances and national fiscal policy, including programs such as the Million Baht Village Fund and the perception of growing indebtedness.

Under a separate agreement, the ministry hired Khun Sombat and his staff as consultants to run the urban survey. Townsend would have access to the resultant data. A conference on the data and collaboration with government economics researchers was also planned. While the new survey might tax an already hard-working staff of enumerators and field editors, Khun Sombat and Townsend saw it as a valuable opportunity to expand the study's scope.

Working from lists provided by the government, TFRP randomly selected 240 households—15 per urban community in each of the existing target provinces: Buriram, Chachoengsao, Lop Buri, Sisaket, Phrae, and Satun. Of the 16 communities to be surveyed in every province, 10 were within capital districts, while the other six were located in the three remaining districts. The survey would also include interviews with village headmen and officials at some local financial institutions, such as the Million Baht Village Fund.

The annual urban survey questionnaire itself would be similar to the annual rural survey, but more business oriented. The rural survey's agricultural focus was irrelevant for many urban households that did not have vegetable plots but rather worked in daily labor or small businesses, such as dry goods shops. This basic difference was the first among many to come. Enumerators and field editors, many of whom had been reviewing the same questionnaires with the same rural households for five years or more, had to adapt in unexpected ways when the urban survey got underway.

Thai towns and cities had their own unique challenges for survey staff, from the growing use of methamphetamine to the mafia-style payoffs that were part of doing business in some places. More subtle cultural and social differences lay beyond the dark news headlines, too. Khun Sombat observed through early interviews that urban Thais tended to marry and start families at a younger age than their rural counterparts. Divorce was more prevalent. More single parents were raising children while running small businesses. Incomes tended to be modest, living expenses were higher, and assistance was scarce, unlike in rural areas, the target of many government aid programs.

This combination of social and economic factors meant urban dwellers were often poorer and more vulnerable to market shifts than rural villagers—a fact that contradicted popular opinion at the time of the survey's launch. The urban survey would, over time, explore this paradox by adding more questions about healthcare and education.

Because urban areas were more business- and commerce oriented than the countryside, many city dwellers would leave home early every morning to open shops, sell in downtown markets, or work in factories. For them, it was nearly impossible to sit down for an interview during working hours. Very early morning and late evening were the only viable times to sift through a questionnaire. And some interviewees—such as government officials, teachers, and police officers—could not even make those times. Weekends were the only dependable free time they had.

To accommodate respondents' work schedules, enumerators visited their shops or places of business, asking questions during small periods of down time, sometimes returning once or twice more to complete the entire survey. Unlike many friendly rural households, where an official letter and a thorough introduction from a village official were enough to gain the trust of interviewees, urban households tended to be more wary. Like their rural counterparts, they too were skeptical about how the data would be used and whether they would see higher taxes as a result. Some wanted to know what was in it for them. Suspicion among neighbors was much higher than in the countryside, and some households wondered what would happen if their financial data got out. Why should they trust the enumerators?

The more heated atmosphere of urban politics and business dealings sometimes led to distrust between government officials and financial institutions. Accusations of corruption and nepotism flew, sometimes complicating survey interviews with bank officials and community savings group directors. In these cases, TFRP was careful to not engage opinions on various political happenings. If a government intervention occurred, such as the Million Baht Village Fund, TFRP would collect information from official committee documents, and enumerators would record how the funds might have impacted the households, so as not to engage opinions about its impact.

For TFRP staff, the urban survey's uncharted territory extended further than they could have imagined. Not only would they have new job descriptions, they would, in some cases, have completely new jobs. Khun Sombat made the unusual decision to substitute field editors and assistant field editors with enumerators for the urban survey. This way, managers could refresh their memories of what it was like to be an enumerator, while enumerators could undergo meaningful real-world training in how to run the surveys. If a field editor chose to leave TFRP, promotions would be easier with a talent pool already trained, and transitions would be smoother.

The job switches would last only for the duration of the urban survey—about 16 working days spread out over two months. Every year, field editors would pick two qualified enumerators who had passed a test. The newly minted editors would earn extra pay, while the field editors-turned-enumerators would continue to carry out their editor duties for the rural monthly survey. Although popular with staff, the experiment did not carry over to the monthly and annual rural surveys. Since those surveys shared the same households, it was decided that it was better to maintain consistency among enumerators and not disrupt established relationships.

Even the urban survey, with all its new techniques and topics, needed consistency. Years of experience had taught Khun Sombat that building trust—to say nothing of managing dozens of employees and a highly detail-oriented project—required steady dependability. It was important for local leaders to know TFRP staff would visit them every summer to coordinate the survey. Field editors needed to know they would receive a budget and basic plan for every fall, and enumerators needed to know they would have a schedule for household interviews well before the survey's start date.

Timing, therefore, was critical to the success of the survey. The annual urban survey coincided with a relatively slow period for the monthly rural survey, as many questions regarding agricultural activity did not apply when fields were fallow. This helped ease the overall burden for enumerators and field editors. Though workloads were limited to no more than two urban surveys per day, staff still worked long hours and enjoyed only short weekends.

Since the first year, with its initial suspicion-laced questions from the households, urban enumerators had managed to establish themselves. As they had in their other survey work, enumerators built trust with consistent and patient explanations, gentle politeness, and occasional small gifts. It was not long before previously taciturn households became chatty, filling the survey's "additional comments" section with all manner of observations and complaints about their lives, their finances, and the region's roads, electricity, and weather.

As he did during the rural surveys, Khun Sombat occasionally stopped in to talk with urban households and review survey questionnaire data. He often met with community leaders during these visits, thanking them for their help and giving gifts such as clocks or drinking glasses emblazoned with TFRP's logo.

As TFRP was trying to develop and maintain a stable system with its new urban survey, the country was teetering on the edge of volatility. By early 2006, unhappiness among elites with Prime Minister Thaksin had led to rumors of an impending coup. The government was in flux and many initiatives, including the Ministry of Finance's funding for the urban survey, would fall by the wayside.

The University of the Thai Chamber of Commerce

In 2004, TFRP's funding from the US federal government was expected to end. A student of Townsend's, on a fellowship from UTCC to the University of Chicago, had relayed to university officials' news of Townsend's desire to continue the survey. Focused on becoming an international center for economic research, UTCC entered into an agreement to fund the monthly surveys while acquiring related data. The young, private Thai university would set up the University of Chicago–UTCC Research Center to more systematically gather secondary data from government ministries and to organize, clean, and disseminate it as widely as possible. This would be a huge step toward the vision of giving international researchers easy access to the Socioeconomic Survey (SES), the Community Development Department (CDD), and other institutions' data. UTCC had also agreed to fund TFRP's monthly rural survey work beginning that same year. After petitioning the university's board of directors for approval, UTCC's

Box 7.1
Political History of Thailand

The Siamese Revolution changed Thailand's governing structure from an absolute monarchy to a constitutional monarchy with then King Prajadhipok's signing of the Constitution of the Siam Kingdom on December 10, 1932. After King Prajadhipok's abdication in 1935, his royal duties were transferred to his nephew and thus continued the reign of the House of Chakri. Since 1932, Thailand has had seventeen constitutions, all of which have been grounded in a constitutional monarchy but which have varied greatly in the role of the judiciary, the military, and civil society. Reigning since 1946, still under the House of Chakri, King Bhumibol Abulyadej is the longest-serving monarch in Thai history.

Following the creation of the role of prime minister in 1932, what had begun as an initiative to end absolutist rule of the monarchy was largely replaced by military rule. Since 1932, most heads of state have been linked to the Royal Thai Army, simultaneously holding the rank of field marshal or general along with their title of prime minister. As recently as the 2006 coup d'état ending Thaksin Shinawatra's tenure as prime minister, the military has sustained its role within the inner workings of the Thai government.

After the military coup that removed him from power, four prime ministers succeeded Thaksin Shinawatra from 2006 to 2008 before the appointment of Abhisit Vejjajiva in 2008. Abhisit Vejjajiva, an economist by training, won the 2008 election with 235 to 198 votes, over Pracha Promnok, the only other candidate running within the National Assembly. Pracha Promnok belonged to the For Thais political party, the same party as the ousted Thaksin Shinawatra. Abhisit Vejjajiva headed the Democratic Party. When he became prime minister at age 44, Abhisit Vejjajiva's relative youth contrasted with the advanced age of his immediate predecessor, Chaovarat Chanweerakul, the acting prime minister who was appointed on December 2, 2008, and served fifteen days in office before being replaced by Abhisit Vejjajiva.

Claiming that Abhisit Vejjajiva took office illegitimately, the United Front for Democracy Against Dictatorship (UDD), commonly referred to as the "Red Shirts," called for a general election to dissolve the Thai parliament. In July of 2011, the Pheu Thai Party, aligned with the UDD, won the general elections, appointing Yingluck Shinawatra as the country's first female prime minister. Prime Minister Yingluck is the sister of the former prime minister, Thaksin Shinawatra. As of July 2012, Prime Minister Yingluck governed as head of a six-party coalition.

president, Chiradet Usawat, announced an initial commitment of 10 million baht, or about 300,000 USD per year.

UTCC continued to pursue opportunities for deepening its involvement with the urban survey. The Thai Project offered not only uniquely valuable information that could contribute to a "library of data," but also provided a closer association with the renowned University of Chicago economics department. UTCC renewed its commitment by pledging another 1.5 million baht, or 45,000 USD per year, for the annual urban survey. It was, Chiradet announced, an important investment in UTCC's future.

Economist James Heckman, Townsend's colleague at the University of Chicago, echoed UTCC's enthusiasm. In a speech celebrating the partnership, Heckman described Townsend's work as the "future" of economics.

As with all new ventures, early missteps needed to be corrected. UTCC's initial system of releasing only 20 percent of funding, followed by installments upon completion of survey phases, made budgeting difficult for Khun Sombat. The university's agreement to clean the data for TFRP proved overly ambitious in the face of the translation difficulties and UTCC staff's lack of familiarity with the survey questionnaires.

Remedies to these problems were identified quickly. TFRP resumed data cleaning activities, and the funding system was reversed so that 80 percent was released at the start and the remaining 20 percent during the course of a survey. Whatever might come, Townsend and TFRP now had a partner they could depend on to support the monthly and urban surveys. The relationship would withstand the military coup that toppled Prime Minister Thaksin in the fall of 2006 and other unforeseen shocks. Keeping a project of this size, scope, and unique approach on track had never been an easy feat. But, once funding was secured, the future seemed brighter.

8 Looking Back: Reflections of a Survey Veteran

After more than a decade of running TFRP in Thailand, Khun Sombat is sanguine about the challenges and payoffs of trying to duplicate the organization's survey work elsewhere. Sitting on the porch of his riverfront home outside Bangkok, he reflects on how the study has survived, how it ensures quality research data, and how it might be recreated outside Thailand.

"Of course," Khun Sombat begins, "you must consider the environments surrounding villages, communities, and society."

No researcher can afford to ignore details such as land, water, and air quality; education; health; fiscal and monetary policy; social networks; culture; tradition; and religion.

"These are known to govern decision making within households and their businesses." But, Khun Sombat cautions, it is a mistake to focus exclusively on these factors. There are other, untold factors that must be taken into account. Without doing so, a study, such as the Townsend Thai Project, would go nowhere.

Communication

First and foremost, he says, there must be good communication and clear knowledge-sharing among the study's directors.

"We have to understand each other," Khun Sombat says of his relationship with Townsend. "It's quite easy for us to communicate because we share knowledge and language of rural economics."

It is a conversation the two collaborators have had continuously since before the beginning of the project. They keep in regular contact by phone and email, and Townsend and Khun Sombat meet in Thailand frequently to examine the project's progress and discuss its direction. During these reviews, the two collaborators talk with study participants and share research results to see if they make sense to the households.

Over the years, Khun Sombat has voiced issues and concerns with Townsend. At one point, for example, Khun Sombat pointed out how onerous a particular survey section could be.

"Khun Sombat explained that tracking down every loan with a baseline loan form was a big burden for someone running a store and selling goods on credit," Townsend recalls. "This part of the questionnaire was taking several days."

So, Townsend scaled back the number of loans enumerators would inquire about, focusing on the largest customers and their respective amounts on credit. It was a compromise that relieved some burden from households while providing representative, if not exhaustive, information.

By keeping open lines of communication, Townsend and Khun Sombat have reduced potential misunderstandings and misinterpretations. Khun Sombat understands what Townsend needs in terms of data variables, and Townsend understands the challenges Khun Sombat faces in the field. "That's how we improve [the study], or how I can adapt it," Khun Sombat says.

The importance of clear and consistent communication, however, extends beyond the study's proponents. In approaching any similar study, Khun Sombat says, researchers and field directors would do well to remember their work is about much more than just numbers and facts scrawled in notebooks.

"As the project goes on, more people—like it or not—will be there along the road the project travels." There are the household interviewees, their relatives, neighbors, local and national officials, politicians, and so on. Survey staff must balance the disparate interests of everyone involved, while maintaining strict objectivity—something Townsend's research depends.

Good communication also involves, of course, good listening. Referring to the tumultuous years following Thaksin's overthrow, Khun Sombat says, "The political situation in Thailand has created a lot of differences between the people. Again, objectivity is key. We have to be in the middle, not get in the middle, and just listen."

It's not always easy to listen. Often, Khun Sombat says, villagers and local leaders will impose upon TFRP staff their opinions on matters only tangentially related to the survey. As with any voicing of opinion, these conversations can become emotional and take up large amounts of time. But they are unavoidable. It's a way of building trust, something neither TFRP's field work nor research can survive without.

Collaboration

For Khun Sombat and Townsend, collaboration has taken many forms since they began TFRP. When considering what is important for academics who wish to pursue a survey of this scope, Townsend stresses the importance of the people. "One has to form teams of people and motivate them, while taking into account culture, customs, and the personal element," says Townsend. "These things cannot be done at a distance and one needs partnerships and indeed close friendships on the ground."

A good example is the time when the prime minister's office summoned Townsend for an accounting of his survey plans and goals. While Townsend was married to a Thai, spoke fluent Thai, and was a disciplined student of the culture, he had never dealt directly with Thai government officials at such a high level. Khun Sombat's extensive government contacts and diplomatic skills proved invaluable.

When plans for a data entry system for the monthly microsurvey bogged down, Townsend turned to Khun Sombat. "It is not exactly my role to create a data system," Khun Sombat says of the experience, but he realized the advantage to developing one in house, where programmers could immediately tackle any data issues that arose. This would ensure higher quality data. "So we had to help him create the system." The result was an efficient program, born of Khun Sombat's keen survey knowledge and unique understanding of Townsend's needs as a researcher.

Similarly, Townsend has been careful to keep close tabs on the multifaceted challenges facing Khun Sombat in the field. This way, Townsend has consistently kept the multi-million-dollar survey operation solvent with well-timed and carefully tailored research grants and other funding vehicles.

Building Relationships

Of course, fieldwork involved relationships beyond just those of Townsend and Khun Sombat. As a way to reiterate how much TFRP values the households, local officials, and others they work with—to create a "friendly feeling," as Khun Sombat puts it—and since the households are not paid to participate in the surveys, enumerators distribute small, inexpensive New Year's gifts every year, as is the Thai tradition. This, too, is a matter of building trust and keeping open lines of communication.

"This study is a really long study. It is many years, and every month we have to interview the households. So we have to create this point [of building rapport with households]," adds Khun Sombat.

To ensure the survey's success, Khun Sombat meets with village leaders prior to the survey to answer any questions or concerns. This not only keeps TFRP staff on schedule so as to survey at consistent times each year, but also builds trust. Indeed, Khun Sombat's relationships with village leaders have helped keep villages and households invested in the survey, lessening attrition. If a household wants to exit the survey, the respective field editor and field supervisor will visit the household to hear concerns and provide additional information on the purpose of the survey. (This isn't always a successful tactic, but the underlying relationships certainly help.)

Inevitably, some families move away or exit the annual and monthly surveys. When this happens, replacement households are randomly selected from a list of households that participated in the respective baseline survey. Attrition rates, or losses of respondents, vary by the survey. For the rural and urban annual resurveys, annual attrition rates are 2.5 percent and 2.6 percent, respectively, and the monthly resurvey has an annualized attrition rate of 1.3 percent. All in all, out of 2,690 households during the years from 1998 to 2002, an average between 15 and 30 households left in a given year. During the years from 2003 to 2007, 39 households were replaced, and from 2008 to 2010 none were replaced.

TFRP staff members play a large role in building these relationships. Beyond the common bond of running a business or farm, staff members can share with locals what it means to be a local. Although they do not work in the villages they live in—to prevent conflicts of interest— enumerators work in the immediate area. This helps reduce the potential for cultural shocks and differences in dialect, customs, religion, or traditions. They share the same living conditions and a common interest in their community's prosperity. Familiarity with local living and working rhythms helps to minimize misunderstandings and maximize clean and thorough data for researchers to cull.

The enumerators know the circumstances of families they interview, and they can relate to many of the challenges the households face. "Many enumerators," Khun Sombat emphasizes, "are operating farms or small businesses just like the villagers." This local advantage allows enumerators to record responses even more accurately, having a solid foundation in the circumstances of the area. Enumerators make sure they comprehend the answers correctly and leave their own opinions or inferences out of the data responses.

Staff members are encouraged to hold second jobs as insurance against the study's possible end and as income to augment their modest salaries. Enumerators run grocery stores, noodle shops, small restaurants, crop farms, fish farms, and beauty salons, among other ventures.

Team leaders help enumerators balance their schedules by making two-month work plans in advance and regularly assessing progress. It's rare that enumerators fall behind these schedules. Khun Sombat recalls one memorable exception—the local man who analyzed soil in Lop Buri for the survey and whose girlfriend "ran away." The man was too bereft to do his job for weeks.

One downside of this local focus is that a staff member who loses his or her job can make things difficult for other enumerators by spreading innuendo about the survey through friends and relatives. A second downside is the potential for hard feelings between the enumerator and a target household. Khun Sombat keeps a close eye on potential conflicts through regular visits with households and local leaders. When problems arise, enumerators are reassigned.

Inevitably, in this process, human nature is at play. This can threaten the integrity of the data. TFRP has set up an administrative structure to prevent errors of misreporting. TFRP now re-interviews and validates a random subsample of the monthly surveys, ranging between 10 and 15 percent, to ensure that responses are accurately recorded.[1] For the annual surveys, the field supervisor will do random checks of key questions in each module. Then, the enumerator will enter the survey response information nightly. If any error notice is received, the enumerator must go back and re-interview the next day.

Investing in Staff

While it might be relatively easy to overlook staff morale in pursuit of survey data, few oversights could be more damaging, Khun Sombat argues. Early on, he instituted core practices promoting egalitarianism, meritocracy, and what he calls "team and family spirit."

While some staff members may have more responsibility or higher salaries, no one is treated as a superior. When teams travel—as some do to assist with work in Satun and Phrae every year—supervisors, field editors, enumerators, and Khun Sombat all share sleeping quarters, meals, and equal per-diem travel allowances. "When we're in the field, we're almost the same," Khun Sombat says. "I think this is part of my nature because I love to do that. I think I can build trust with my staff because of that."

To further morale, every year, a small portion of TFRP's operating budget goes toward a group vacation. Staff members and their families are invited to a peaceful beach or mountain resort, where they play games and discuss their field work. It's a matter of building bonds within and among teams, facilitating more open communication, sharing thoughts and suggestions. As Khun Sombat puts it simply, "We create relationships."

Survey work is often lonely, unsteady, and low paying. To give staff a sense of belonging and investment in the project, Khun Sombat set up a voluntary group mutual fund. He deducted 3 percent from participants' salaries, while adding an equal amount in their names to the fund. It was not exactly popular at first. "Many of them said they want to use the money. But after two years, three years, they saw the others start to have big savings, so they came over." These days, an elected committee of staff members runs the 1.3 million baht or 39,000 USD fund and makes intrastaff loan decisions. The fund averages a 4 percent annual return.

Planning and Adaptation

Like many projects that evolve as time passes, the Townsend Thai surveys look different now than in their beginnings. New challenges and opportunities in the field shape the surveys, and new questions have created the need for expanded questionnaires and survey areas.

When Townsend and Khun Sombat set out to field the baseline survey in 1997, they anticipated that having a large cross-section of villages would reveal the variations in the financial system. For example, they hoped to discover the impact of existing informal institutions, such as gift giving, and more formal institutions, such as commercial and government banks.

Looking back, Townsend admits that this was an overly ambitious design. With the financial crisis, the environment was no longer constant. It became clear that a longer-run panel data—with a smaller sample—was necessary to answer the questions the team sought to answer.

In data collection, it can be difficult to anticipate future events that may have an impact on the population being studied. Decisions have to be made as events unfold. At the same time, there can be great value in dedicating research efforts to a longer panel that can be expanded and modified as circumstances vary. The effect of varied and unforeseen circumstances can be seen in changes made to the Townsend Thai surveys over time: the scope evolved to include urban areas as industrialization spread, political unrest ended data collection in Yala, and new skill-based questions were incorporated to understand the performance of entrepreneurs. As Thailand grew and adapted, so did the survey.

Confronting Crossroads and Culture

Along the way, Townsend and the team reached various crossroads, where decisions had to be made and trade-offs were inevitable. For example, it was common knowledge that many of the households kept gold and jewelry in the house. Asking directly about these holdings could easily create mistrust between households and the survey staff or, worse, result in the household exiting the survey. So it was determined that questions about jewelry and gold should be excluded. Not having this information created gaps in the reporting of assets or savings. This was one side effect of avoiding intimate questions about wealth.

More recently, data summaries showed that many farmers hoarded cash in their houses instead of putting it in banks. To find out why, Townsend joined the enumerators in the summer of 2008. "It's crucial for the research," Townsend noted. Khun Sombat also joined the quest, renewing a conversation that began in Lop Buri several years earlier. Some farmers there were holding cash close in case of sudden emergencies that might require fast payments of large sums. Some feared saving with banks might lead to third parties learning about their relative wealth. To more accurately get at the reasons, Khun Sombat and Townsend worked up a series of questions to add to the formal instruments. They also planned to check the measurements of cash by combining statistical codes, developed in Chicago, with the data entry system in the field.

Regardless of their reasons, most of the farmers hoarding cash seemed unconcerned with losing their money to a home break in. "We asked, are you worried about robbery?" Khun Sombat recalls with a laugh. "They said, 'No, because we have guns.'"

The team was optimistic when determining the monthly survey questions. Asking such detailed questions on daily and weekly financial activities could easily be perceived as overly intrusive and tedious. Graceful oversight on the part of Khun Sombat, however, coupled with willingness on the part of households to track and report such information, has validated the initial optimism and provided invaluable data for analysis. Today, this carefully worded and organized set of questions enables Townsend and the research team to create detailed financial accounts, such as balance sheets and cash flow statements. For example, the team has developed frameworks for measuring income and consumption and distinguishing liquidity from productivity when examining household businesses. This type of analysis would not be possible without well-designed and closely tailored survey instruments.

Promises Detract from Purpose

Khun Sombat and Townsend also recognize that building trust between enumerators and households is important, but there is danger in getting too close and offering too much help. In order to ensure cooperation in these situations, some research projects make upfront promises to their interview subjects, assuring them that their participation will help bring government aid or grant money from nongovernmental organizations. This, Khun Sombat says, is not only a fatal error for a long-term study such as TFRP but also potentially misleading, even if it is true.

If the benefits promised are not realized, villagers are likely to lose trust and respect for the study. And, even if aid money or other promised benefits materialize, they may not be appropriate for their situation and, in the end, they could be considered unhelpful.

Khun Sombat recalls such a case when he was working on a study for the BAAC. Donor countries, including Germany, Japan, and the United States had specified the study would run for four to five months. At that point, funding would be released, with the objective of raising incomes and bettering living standards.

The problem, Khun Sombat says, is that a few months is rarely enough time to gather an accurate picture of what a community is grappling with and what it needs to succeed. "That promise [of improving living standards] would become a big disaster to the research project if it could not be fulfilled."

Townsend shares a similar story from his early years in northern Thailand. At the time, per capita income seemed to be increasing in a region targeted by a USAID project. On second look, however, the gains appeared unsustainable, wholly dependent on the project's aid funding salaries being paid.

Everyone involved in a large scale survey, such as TFRP, needs to understand that the survey is first and foremost about rigorous academic research. The research it leads to may someday shape government policy, but that is a hope, not a guarantee. Until then, the survey's focus should be solely on factors—such as supply, demand, labor, capital, land, goods, and services—that affect individual decisions and the function of villages, counties, and the nation. The research's focus is on producing detailed and accurate information about household-level economies, and to understand the process of development and what it means for average people. Only then can researchers offer insight into how government policies might be adjusted for regional differences.

Khun Sombat puts it this way: "If there is no true research, no true study in the life of the farm households or villagers for a long time, you cannot create an effective project."

As with any healthy relationship, Khun Sombat says, a successful study like TFRP must steer clear of conflicts and unfulfilled promises. To that end, he insists that survey staff members should always identify themselves as researchers focused on learning how villagers deal with changes in the environments surrounding them. Survey staff members are not organizers. They have to make clear that their focus is not to create an aid project.

TFRP enumerators are instructed to discuss the study's academic aspects rather than any potential impact on government policy or agency funding. Even if an aspect of the study has direct ties to a funding program, as is the case with TFRP, enumerators do not discuss it.

Some respondents, however, maintain the expectation of a reward for participating in the survey. Local officials have often queried Khun Sombat and his staff at length about the study's potential for benefiting their communities. They've often inquired about its political ties and implications. The simple answer, Khun Sombat says, is that there is nothing political about TFRP—no political motives, influences, or conflicts.

"Many people were waiting for the outcome," Khun Sombat says of TFRP's early work. "So we had to start a dialogue with the government agencies and the universities, to make sure they understand this study is real academic research. We want people to understand the value of this research."

The Way Forward

With so much invested in TFRP's survey work, Khun Sombat and Townsend can scarcely imagine a future without the study and its many challenges.

Some heads of target households have died. Their children may not, in some cases, be interested in continuing with the survey. They may move away. "Recently, we started talking with every household that has kids," Khun Sombat says. "We found out that many of them are going to leave the farm and move to town because they have a job there."

Seeing the shifting landscape, with many villagers migrating from rural communities to urban and industrial centers, Townsend realized the need for the urban survey. But while the survey has collected a notable amount of data, it cannot recover or track the exiting households of past years. Having learned this hard lesson, Townsend and the team are formulating plans to track migrant families with cell phones, a resource that was not available when the survey started.

Going forward, they will also more thoroughly measure skills, attitudes, and overall well-being—metrics that will complement economic models' estimates in the research. What skills are of advantage to migrants? Is enhanced secondary education valuable for everyone? Questions like these, based on lessons learned from ongoing research into topics, such as health decisions, will be incorporated into data gathering.

"Our questionnaires still hold the capability to assess changes in the surveyed households," Khun Sombat says. "But do we need to revise, delete, or add some things? How should we do it?"

Dissertations at the University of Chicago, based on the data, have led to a systematic list of ways to improve the questionnaire. Ineffectual questions in all the instruments are eventually discarded from the survey. Other answers pertaining to the survey have yet to be found.

That, Khun Sombat says, is the nature of the work. It is the nature of studying how people—fickle, ever changing, and unpredictable—live.

"Before this project," he says, "I thought there were many things we could tell people about managing their money and creating stimulus. But money is not everything." The survey work is not, at base, about money or individuals, Khun Sombat says. "It's not just one person, but their father, their mother, their children, their neighbors."

Together, these reflections show the evolving nature of the Townsend Thai Project. Faced with challenges in data collection and changing economic and social landscapes, the team adapts and identifies solutions. This pattern continues to repeat itself, as the surveys get fielded year after year, province by province. Townsend and Khun Sombat continue to learn, too.

Epilogue: Research Findings and Policy Recommendations

As highlighted throughout this book, the Townsend Thai Data are extensive and provide a unique snapshot of Thai life and transition over time. The combination of both annual and monthly data provides a comprehensive overview of how families change, adapt, manage adverse events, handle risk, invest, grow, and thrive. Through the data, we can follow the life trajectories of thousands of different households, both rural and urban, both rich and poor.

These data allow us to track how families deal with the good times and the bad. When families do well, we can see how they save or invest in themselves, their children, or a business. Our data allow us to track if and how these kinds of investments pay off for the families. When times are bad, we see how households cope and get by through borrowing money from friends, family members, and banks. In some cases, we see people who struggle without any kind of support system, and as a result are more vulnerable than others.

While even simple summaries of the data such as these are worthwhile in providing insights into how families and their activities change over time, the project has gone far beyond summarizing data to assess how well the financial system is working overall. Doing this analysis well requires economic models, which allow us to see how all of the economy—markets, institutions, and policy—is currently put together. One family of models, general equilibrium models, specifies the underlying environment of the economy by using data from the surveys. Economic theory is then used to set expectations of what ideal outcomes should be; that is to say, such theory helps establish *benchmark standards*. We can then test whether the financial system is operating efficiently or not.

These models are useful for policy analysis in three primary ways. First, we can evaluate the efficiency of policy outcomes and assess the impact of current policies within an economy. Second, we can assess new and potential innovations and how they might affect individuals, households, and firms within the economy. Finally, we can use models to design better markets, regulatory mechanisms, and macroeconomic policy.

The use of general equilibrium models is important because they provide a framework in which all the pieces of the economy can be connected, logically and methodically. That framework allows us to operate "from the ground up," from households to villages to the national level, and "from the top down," from national events, such as a financial crisis, to households. Indeed, the Townsend Thai Data have proved essential in understanding events and evaluating policies across many levels of analyses. Here, we highlight some of the more salient findings and promising avenues of investigation stemming from this rich data source.

Village Economies

The Townsend Thai Data provide us with a great deal of information at the village and community level. Villages can be interesting to study from a policy perspective, and this is particularly true in Thailand because many policies are implemented at the village level and, in many instances, households within a village are closely connected to one another.

Risk, Shocks, and Insurance

Our research starts by looking at how villages are doing on their own in terms of how they handle adverse events. Risk is the level to which a household may suffer from shocks, which are notable events that can negatively impact a household's financial well-being. Within a village, there is a diversity of incomes across households. For example, some households consist of wage laborers, while members of other households run farms and businesses. Each of these occupations carries a different level of risk, so not everyone is impacted equally by common, village-level shocks. For instance, a shock might be a drought, which would affect farmers. Other shocks, like a flood, affect an entire village (or region or country, for that matter), while yet others only affect one household or one individual, like an unexpected illness or disability.

We then evaluate how individual-level shocks within a village should be pooled, or put together, and how village-level shocks should be shared. For instance, in order to financially weather a shock, extended family members might lend money in order to help their relatives through the difficult time. In essence, there is insurance across households. Just as someone in the United States might rely on auto insurance in anticipation of the chance of an accident, villagers find insurance in receiving assistance from their fellow neighbors or family members in the time of an unexpected event.

Perhaps surprisingly, our research finds that most villages share risk quite well, and even optimally.[1] This is particularly true if we look at households whose members have other extended family in the village and form informal kinship networks, or networks of family or friends who can be called upon in a time of need. Such households do not need to be provided with within-village insurance products because they have the benefit of accessing help via their relationships. These kinds of arrangements can be considered informal markets, in contrast with more formal markets, like a commercial business selling an insurance product to a customer, as is often the case in the United States. We find that there is more going on within villages' informal markets than may be suspected, and that the government should not attempt to eliminate these efficient, informal risk-sharing arrangements.

On the other hand, if we look at low-wealth households who are not part of kinship networks, we find that they are much more vulnerable to income shocks. Thus, policy should be directed toward providing these households with insurance. What would such a policy look like? Economic theory tells us that all households within a village could be made better off if the intervention is internal to the village. In this type of intervention, the better-insured and less risk-averse households (those who have access to help from kin) would provide insurance to their less fortunate neighbors and, in principle, make reasonable but nonexploitative profits doing it. Of course, successful implementation would require finding expertise on organizing the community.

It is worth noting that providing good insurance at the local level does not mean providing full insurance, or completely eliminating losses from adverse events. Indeed, common village-level risks cannot be eliminated. Our research finds that there is substantial variation in how willing different households are to be exposed to this common risk.[2] While some households are very conservative and choose to limit their exposure to financial risk, others are more aggressive in making choices that might carry significant financial risk. Interestingly, the willingness of households to take risks is not related to wealth. So, some relatively poor households do supply insurance within the village through kinship networks. These nuances must be taken into account when considering policy solutions.

Return on Assets and Intermediation

Unfortunately, when we examine opportunities for saving and investing, our research indicates that there is much room for improvement within villages. For this analysis, we look primarily at the rate of return on assets (ROA). ROA is defined as the productivity, or the stream of output, that results from a collection of productive assets.

Households with a high ROA, or those with greater output for every asset owned, are more actively involved in the formal financial system through the use of savings accounts and loans. Interestingly, households with a high ROA save larger amounts, save at a higher rate, and put more of those savings into their own business. Households thus confirm through their own actions that the benefit of using their capital to grow their businesses is higher than alternative uses of the funds. These households know how to save effectively and where to put their money.

However, households with a high ROA are limited because they are not getting much money from others. They do not typically receive informal credit from their village neighbors, or, if they do, it is typically insufficient. This ends up being detrimental for all households in the village. This is because there are households with a low ROA who are not investing in their neighbors' businesses and are thus receiving lower returns on their funds than might be possible. Therefore, interventions should focus on encouraging the flow of savings and loans within the village.

Microfinance Interventions

The longevity of the data has provided unique opportunities to evaluate actual policy changes. One intervention we have examined closely is a government microfinance initiative called the Million Baht Fund, which was launched in 2002. The fund seeded approximately $24,000 to capitalize a local fund for each village in Thailand in order to provide credit and stimulate local economies. This added up to 1.5 percent of gross domestic product (GDP) and is arguably one of the world's largest microfinance interventions. If we want to know what impact microfinance might have in the future, this is the obvious starting point.

Within villages, our research on the fund shows increased consumption of goods and services, profits from business, wages paid for construction, labor income, agricultural investment, and total borrowing.[3] At the same time, the data indicate that default rates on credit increased and financial savings decreased.

Indeed, in the data, we can see one set of households with low levels of cash which increased consumption with the additional flows of money. A second set of households with increased consumption also shows up in the data, but these households consumed more because they thought they could more easily obtain credit during hard times in the future, with the advent of the fund. These households effectively cashed in their financial savings. Some households that were contemplating large investment opportunities, however, lowered consumption and used the additional credit to make that investment.

Other research yields indications that the fund's money largely made its way, within each village, to those households with a high ROA, exactly as we might have hoped.[4] Thus, the microfinance intervention offered a partial remedy to some kind of market failure, or to the lack of flows from savers to borrowers.

Overall, research suggests that village funds may need to be strengthened and are not always the solution to insufficient local financial systems. Across rural villages, loan repayment is found to be positively associated with the quality of institutions in rural areas, meaning that repayments are higher in areas where the local financial institutions are stronger.[5] Households in rural areas thus have some knowledge about local customs or characteristics that vary across communities and effectively predicted, in their answers to our initial 1997 surveys, the eventual success or failure of the microfinance programs launched in 2002. Yet this result only holds in rural areas. Solicited ratings have little correlation in towns. On the other hand, the strength of social sanctions is positively correlated with repayment in both rural and urban areas. As the ability to enforce sanctions varies, so does the success of these funds.

Regional Variation

Given this extensive information at the village level, we can then focus on regional divisions in Thailand and compare across villages and provinces. One way to approach this comparison is through a framework that views villages as "small open economies."[6] That is, we argue that villages and regions are not closed in trade or financial links, but rather like countries in the world economy: They are open to regional trade and to flows of currency and credit. Using this framework, the relationships across villages can be studied in the same way that international economists analyze the economies of nations and the interactions among them.

As in many developing countries, there is substantial variation in occupations, income, wealth, and rates of poverty across different regions and urban and rural areas in Thailand. Here we see evidence of significant economic activity at the inter- and intraregional level. For example, we discover that cash is used more across villages than within villages. Borrowing is also more prevalent across villages than within villages, reflecting the dominance of formal rather than informal sources at the national level. Similarly, gifts and lending diminish at the regional level, as these were presumably driven previously by informal money markets within villages. Remittances, though, do play a large and growing role at the regional and national levels.

Financial Systems and Bank Location

Analysis at a regional level is particularly valuable in examining differences within the formal financial system across provinces. Research in this area has followed several tracks. To begin, we look at geographic aspects of Thailand's financial systems, such as bank branch locations. We identify participation rates in the financial system and find that the financial system has not expanded as it should, even taking into account constraints associated with limited wealth.[7] One hypothesis for this is that banks may view towns and cities as areas for bank branches to mobilize deposits but do not see nearby villages as opportunities for lending. It is not that banks are not lending at all, but rather, they are lending too little to achieve efficiency.

When we look more closely at branch location data, we see clustering of commercial banks in and around Bangkok and in selected subareas of provinces. For the most part, banks are building on top of existing commercial banks. The government's Bank for Agriculture and Agricultural Cooperatives (BAAC), in contrast, systematically extends its branch network and tends to locate in less-connected, smaller villages. The reasons for this clustering are being examined in ongoing research.[8]

A second main area of research in the evaluation of regional financial systems is the use of institutional scorecards. From data gathered on financial institutions, we have created an assessment that evaluates institutions according to how well they serve the public in reducing financial risk by facilitating saving and lending across villages. Research shows that the BAAC does quite well in keeping both consumption and investment consistent, even amid shocks.[9] This is likely because loans made by the BAAC allow for deferred payment and restructuring in the event of shocks. Commercial banks also do well by this metric, though it seems that commercial loans in rural areas are sparse and savings accounts are more commonly used. Interestingly, village-level production credit groups and regional agricultural cooperatives do much less well or are entirely ineffective. In summary, this scoring system ultimately could be formalized to measure the quality of financial access, hence developing more efficient financial systems.

Financial Access: Putting the Pieces Together
Access to financial services such as savings, insurance, and credit is important, but do all individuals need to be directly connected to a financial institution? Using the data, we have been able to map all of the financial connections via gifts and loans within a village.[10] We find that being indirectly linked through informal, village-level networks to a BAAC or commercial bank is just as effective for consumption smoothing and the timing of investment as being a direct customer. This reinforces the earlier findings that those with family and networks do well against village shocks, but those without direct or indirect access through kinship networks are quite vulnerable.[11] This latter group loses not only the network but also the benefit of indirect access to outside formal financial institutions.

Two conclusions follow from this. First, measured financial access can be a misleading indicator of actual financial access because access through the local village network is not counted. Second, formal and informal systems are complementary. One of the ways in which this works is that loans that are owed to a national-level financial-sector provider are sometimes paid off by a chain of informal transactions at the village-level.[12] Elimination of the informal sector could hamper these institutions or cause default, among other related problems. In its own way, shadow banking, in this rural context, is a good thing.

Overall, the cross-village comparisons and regional analyses make clear that banking and microfinance have the capability of transforming entire areas, lifting many people out of poverty. It is also a way, through the lens of economic models, to assess the role that various

types of institutions are playing, picking up inconsistencies or ineffi-
ciencies that might be eliminated through appropriate policy or prevent
welfare loses that result from inappropriate policies.

National Level

With data in hand, we can more richly assess what is happening at the
household, village, and regional levels, and we find greater opportunity for assessing the financial systems at the national level. That is, we
can look from households to the national level, or "from the bottom
up," and from national events, such as a financial crisis, to households,
or "from the top down."

There are two common (and particularly notable) misconceptions
when moving from household-level data to aggregated data for the
entire country. One is that small businesses, however numerous, don't
matter for national income or productivity. This is simply not the case.
Data shows that income from nonfarm businesses easily dominates
corporate profits and is the second most important contributor to
national income. The second misconception is that only large financial
institutions really matter, that government banks and microfinance
have to do with social programs and equity and not with GDP. It is
true that at the national level, the number of bank branches, assets
accumulated, funds mobilized, and credit extended is dominated by
commercial banks. But this is much less the case in provinces where
the BAAC dominates the formal sector. Moreover, the informal sector
via village funds is found to be quite large and, in rural areas, is still
the single largest segment. As we have seen in the data, BAAC and
village funds and networks are movers of income and growth.

Flow of Funds

One of the ways in which the data has been particularly useful for
analyses at a national level is by providing detailed, household- and
regional-level information on Thailand's flow of funds. Flow of funds
accounts (FFA) capture the flows of money among households, businesses, financial institutions, and governments in a country. The
accounts are important because they allow a mapping of primary financial relationships within a financial system.

As discussed in several previous chapters, a developing country's
financial system ought to achieve efficiency as evidenced by ideal
insurance and the effective access to opportunities for saving and

lending, for example. The challenge is that it can be difficult to determine how well financial markets and institutions function in practice. The typical practice is to write down macroeconomic and monetary models without actually looking closely at the underlying transactions. However, the Thai surveys, along with other trends in economics (the 2008 US financial crisis being one of them), have given impetus to better measurement. A notable goal, therefore, is to begin establishing the framework for creating FFA for Thailand.

We are particularly interested in whether and how low-wealth households save, interact with, and are affected by financial systems. FFA typically follow the national income accounts in distinguishing firms, households, governments, and the rest of the world, but they usually do not attempt to split households by wealth level, for example, or geography. As a result, the savings situation of low-wealth households, and what is going on in villages or urban communities, is likely to be obscured in the aggregate data. We are in the process of creating FFA at the village level,[13] and we are making plans to collaborate with the Thai government in using the Townsend Thai Data, a new survey on small business which we have supported, and other existing secondary data to improve flow of funds accounting.

Conclusion

The importance of the Townsend Thai Data cannot be limited to these pages alone. The data are evergreen and continue to yield new and significant findings. Longevity has been the most notable characteristic of the data, with no other developing country having such extensive panel data. Researchers around the world interact with the data on a daily basis, producing findings that hold importance for Thailand and the world.

None of these findings, however, could have been possible without the relationships and people described in this book. From the trust of the households to the diplomacy of the staff, the data themselves are a testament to the cooperation of all those involved. The hope is that what has been found can better the lives of those in Thailand over the years to come and provide a model and motivation for similar work elsewhere in the world.

Appendix

The following pages contain a list of research conducted using the Townsend Thai Data. These publications are listed according to topic and are accompanied by abstracts that appeared in the original.

Village Economies and Household Firms

Robert M. Townsend and Krislert Samphantharak, "Measuring the Return on Household Enterprise: What Matters Most for Whom?" *Journal of Development Economics* 98, no. 1 (2012): 58–70.

Return on assets (ROA) from household enterprise is crucial for understanding the well-being and productivity of households in developing economies. Yet the definition and measurement of household enterprise ROA remain inconsistent or unclear. We illustrate potential measurement problems with examples from various actual surveys. We then take advantage of a detailed integrated household survey to perform a robustness analysis, acting as if we had gathered less data than was actually the case, to see what matters and for whom. The three issues that matter most for accurate measurement of household enterprise ROA are the choice of accrual versus cash basis of income, the treatment of households' own labor in enterprise income, and the treatment of non-factor income. Also, this sensitivity matters most for a relatively poor region dominated by crop cultivation relative to a richer region with non-farm enterprises. Though the choice between accrued income and cash income matters less when the frequency of the data declines, there remains high sensitivity in longer-term and annualized data. We conclude the paper by providing recommendations on how to improve the survey questionnaires for more accurate measurement in field research.

Archawa Paweenawat and Robert M. Townsend, "Villages as Small Open Economies" (working paper, 2011).

We propose a framework to generate village economic accounts and village balance of payments accounts from a micro-level household survey. Using the Townsend Thai Data, we create the village economic and balance of payments accounts of rural villages in Thailand. We then study village economies through the lens of international economics, both real and financial. These include the Feldstein–Horioka puzzle; openness and growth; across countries risk sharing; the factor-price equalization; trade, capital flows, and financial frictions; trade and productivity.

Robert M. Townsend and Krislert Samphantharak, "Households as Corporate Firms: An Analysis of Household Finance Using Integrated Household Surveys and Corporate Financial Accounting," *Econometric Society Monograph Series* 46, (December 2009).

This investigation proposes a conceptual framework for measurement necessary for an analysis of household finance and economic development. The authors build on and, where appropriate, modify corporate financial accounts to create balance sheets, income statements, and statements of cash flows for households in developing countries, using an integrated household survey. The authors also illustrate how to apply the accounts to an analysis of household finance that includes productivity of household enterprises, capital structure, liquidity, financing, and portfolio management. The conceptualization of this analysis has important implications for measurement, questionnaire design, the modeling of household decisions, and the analysis of panel data.

Robert M. Townsend, "Financial Systems in Northern Thai Villages," *Quarterly Journal of Economics* 110, no. 4 (November 1995): 1011–1046.

Field research attempted to measure the risky environments, the information structures, the institutions, and the risk-response mechanisms of ten villages in northern Thailand. Various key features are then modeled in an abstract but realistic way, either with a full-information risk-sharing model or an information-constrained version of the same model. Observations from some of the villages seem consistent with one or the other of these models, but in many of the villages, one is left with risk-response variations across households which suggest that Pareto improvements are possible.

Robert M. Townsend. "Understanding the Structure of Village and Regional Economies," in *Contract Economies*, eds. Lars Werin and Hans Wijkander (Oxford, UK: Basil Blackwell, 1992), 114–148.

This chapter takes a contract-theoretic, mechanism-design approach in trying to understand the structure of entire economies. That is, markets, institutions, and allocations are viewed as Pareto-optimal given the environments of the economies, possibly restricted by private information and incentive problems. The jump from the usual applications of contract theory, namely two (or a small number of) agent problems, to entire economies may make this endeavor seem an implausible enterprise. But for observational and theoretical reasons, the enterprise is replete with possibilities for a greater understanding of the determinants of contract structure in general and for the structure of selected economies in particular. A second layer of the analysis considers villages as part of larger regional economies and asks again whether arrangements appear to be efficient. Some but not all of the arguments for plausibility apply at the regional level as well.

Credit, Intermediation, and Microfinance

Joseph P. Kaboski and Robert M. Townsend, "The Impacts of Credit on Village Economies," *American Economic Journal: Applied Economics* 4, no. 2 (April 2012): 98–133.

This paper evaluates the short-term impact of Thailand's Million Baht Village Fund program, among the largest scale government microfinance initiative in the world, using pre- and post-program panel data and quasi-experimental cross-village variation in credit-per-household. We find that the village funds have increased total short-term credit, consumption, agricultural investment, income growth (from business and labor), but decreased overall asset growth. We also find a positive impact on wages, an important general equilibrium effect. The findings are broadly consistent qualitatively with models of credit-constrained household behavior and models of intermediation and growth.

Joseph P. Kaboski and Robert M. Townsend, "A Structural Evaluation of a Large-Scale Quasi-Experimental Microfinance Initiative," *Econometrica* 79, no. 5 (2011): 1357–1406.

This paper uses a structural model to understand, predict, and evaluate the impact of an exogenous microcredit intervention program, the Thai Million Baht Village Fund program. We model household decisions in the face of borrowing constraints, income uncertainty, and high-yield indivisible investment opportunities. After estimation of parameters using pre-program data, we evaluate the model's ability to predict and interpret the impact of the village fund intervention. Simulations from the model mirror the data in yielding a greater increase in consumption than credit, which is interpreted as evidence of credit constraints. A cost–benefit analysis using the model indicates that some households value the program much more than its per household cost, but overall the program costs 20 percent more than the sum of these benefits.

Xavier Giné, "Access to Capital in Rural Thailand: An Estimated Model of Formal vs. Informal Credit," *Journal of Development Economics* 96, (2011): 16–29.

This paper tries to understand the mechanism underlying access to credit. We focus on two important aspects of rural credit markets. First, moneylenders and other informal lenders coexist with formal lending institutions such as government or commercial banks, and more recently, micro-lending institutions. Second, potential borrowers presumably face sizable transaction costs obtaining external credit. We develop and estimate a model based on limited enforcement and transaction costs that provides a unified view of these facts. Using data from Thailand, the results show that the limited ability of banks to enforce contracts, more than transaction costs, is crucial in understanding the observed diversity of lenders.

Adriana de la Huerta, "Microfinance in Rural and Urban Thailand: Policies, Social Ties and Successful Performance" (PhD diss., University of Chicago, 2011).

It has been well documented in the theoretical economic literature that joint liability group-based lending helps to overcome the hurdles of adverse selection, moral hazard, auditing cost and enforcement by exploiting local information embodied in specific social networks. Much less attention has been given to explain how other features of microcredit contracts have opened up possibilities for microfinance. In this paper I study a joint liability lending program in Thailand to analyze how social ties and policies such as compulsory savings and training contribute to explain the success of the program in terms of repayment rates in rural and urban communities. I use a novel panel dataset on household loans constructed from household, institutional and community-level data from the Townsend Thai Data. Empirical results are consistent with the repayment predictions of existing theories on joint liability lending. The findings suggest that joint liability may prosper in areas in which social ties are strong enough to permit individuals to costlessly enforce agreements in their community, and the threat of social sanctions exists and is credible. Additionally, I find evidence that suggests that households in rural areas have some knowledge about the customs and characteristics of people and institutions in the region which varies across communities and predicts success and failure of the microfinance program. The estimation results also indicate that the degree of joint liability in the fund is negatively associated with repayment; and that practices such as requiring compulsory savings and providing training or information to borrowers are positive predictors of repayment in both rural and urban environments. The findings are robust to a number of specification checks.

Christian Ahlin and Robert M. Townsend, "Selection into and across Credit Contracts: Theory and Field Research," *Journal of Econometrics* 136, no. 2 (February 2007): 665–698.

Lenders may choose to encourage borrower side contracting using group, or cosigned, loans or discourage it using individual loans, so as to make relative performance comparisons. In this context wealth of the agents relative to outsiders, and wealth inequality among potential joint liability partners, are important factors determining the choice among loan contracts. In a related model of whether to borrow, higher covariance of returns mitigates an adverse selection effect. We test these models using relatively rich data gathered in field research in Thailand. The prevalence of joint liability contracts relative to individual contracts exhibits a U-shaped relationship with the wealth of the borrowing household and increases with the wealth dispersion. The likelihood of joint-liability borrowing increases the lower is the probability of project success, a direct affirmation of adverse selection. Higher correlation across projects makes joint liability borrowing more likely relative to all other alternatives. Strikingly, most of the results disappear if we do not condition the sample according to the dictates of the models, with selection into and across credit contracts.

Christian Ahlin and Robert M. Townsend, "Using Repayment Data to Test Across Models of Joint Liability Lending," *Economic Journal* 117, no. 517 (March 2007): F11–F51.B63.

Theories rationalizing joint liability lending are rich in implications for repayment rates. We exploit this fact to test four diverse models. We show that the models' repayment implications do not always coincide. For example, higher correlation of output and borrowers' ability to act cooperatively can raise or lower repayment, depending on the model. Data from Thai borrowing groups suggest that repayment is affected negatively by the joint liability rate (ceteris paribus) and social ties, and positively by the strength of local sanctions and correlated returns. Further, the relative fit of the adverse selection versus informal sanctions models varies by region.

Robert M. Townsend. "Credit, Intermediation and Poverty Reduction," in *Understanding Poverty*, eds. Abhijit Banerjee, Roland Benabou, and Dilip Mookherjee (New York: Oxford University Press, 2006).

The purpose of this essay is to show how credit markets influence development and to argue that the impact of improvements in credit markets is quantitatively significant. The essay first establishes the fact that access to credit is limited, emphasizing the magnitudes. It then goes on to the potential importance of financial sector development, again quantifying the impact. Toward the end of the essay there is a discussion of the merits of different interventions.

The policy recommendations in this essay are based on estimated versions of the Thai reality, filtered through the lens of artificial environments, or what economists call models. For example to understand what the effect of financial development we create an artificial environment that is structured to imitate key aspects of Thailand in this period, where we let financial development take place Further, as the logic of the model is made explicit, one can trace a particular recommendation to a given set of assumptions or rules. In Thailand, where this research is being conducted, with the aid of much data gathered in field research, specific and concrete policy advice can be given.

Joseph P. Kaboski and Robert M. Townsend, "Policies and Impact: An Evaluation of Village-Level Microfinance Institutions," *Journal of the European Economic Association* 3, no. 1 (January 2005): 1–50.

This paper uses variation in policies and institutional characteristics to evaluate the impacts of village-level microfinance institutions in rural Thailand. To identify impacts, we use policies related to the successful/unsuccessful provision of services as exogenous variation in effective financial intermediation. We find that institutions, particularly those with good policies, can promote asset growth, consumption smoothing and occupational mobility, and can decrease moneylender reliance. Specifically, cash-lending institutions—production credit groups and especially women's groups—are successful in providing intermediation and its benefits to members, while buffalo banks and rice banks are not. The policies identified as important to intermediation and benefits: the provision of savings services, especially pledged savings accounts; emergency services; and training and advice. Surprisingly, much publicized policies such as joint liability, default consequences, or repayment frequency had no measured impacts.

Robert M. Townsend., "Micro Credit and Mechanism Design," *Journal of the European Economic Association* 1, no. 2–3 (April–May 2003): 468–477.

Individual microcredit loans are not necessarily simple fixed debt obligations, but rather may have contingencies and procedures suggested by the theory of mechanism design. Further, group or joint-liability lending may not be the single miracle cure practitioners claim nor operate the way the logic of a single theory might suggest. There are multiple theories, these theories can be distinguished in data on repayment rates, and the best-fit theory may vary with the environment. Finally, the debate about whether to lend to individuals or lend to groups may be misplaced. Under simple theories of selection, the Pareto superior regime, which is predicted to emerge, varies with exogenous environmental characteristics.

Climate and Geography

John Felkner and Robert M. Townsend, "The Geographic Concentration of Enterprise in Developing Countries," *Quarterly Journal of Economics* 126, no. 4 (2011): 2005–2061.

A nation's economic geography can have an enormous impact on its development. In Thailand, we show that a high concentration of enterprise in an area predicts high subsequent growth in and around that area. We also find spatially contiguous convergence of enterprise with stagnant areas left behind. Exogenous physiographic conditions are correlated with enterprise location and growth. We fit a structural, micro-founded model of occupation transitions with fine-tuned geographic capabilities to village data and replicate these salient facts. Key elements of the model include costs, credit constraints on occupation choice, and spatially varying expansion of financial service providers.

Kamilya Tazhibayeva, "Empirical Essays in Development Economics" (PhD diss., University of Chicago, 2011).

This dissertation consists of two essays on decision making of individuals in developing economies with regards to earning opportunities. The common underlying theme is empirical analysis of processes which have large potential to affect individual earnings in developing economies: human capital accumulation (chapter 1) and production adjustments by traditional farmers to potential climate change (chapter 2). Chapter 2 (joint with Professor Robert Townsend from MIT and John Felkner from the National Opinion Research Center) models production behavior of rice growing farmers in Thailand and accesses their ability to adjust to different climate change scenarios. We specify a three-stage production function for rice cultivation which incorporates the sequential nature of both production shocks realizations, including rainfall, and input choices which are based on sequentially updated information sets of history of realized shocks and observed changes in crop growth. We integrate our economic model of rice production with soil science crop growth modeling, weather simulators, and global climate change models. We consider two alternative climate change scenarios for Southeast Asia. Comparison of yield changes predicted by the soil science model, which does not account for adjustments in input usage, with economic model predictions demonstrates the extent of farmers' ability to mitigate adverse effects of climate change.

John Felkner, Kamilya Tazhibayeva, and Robert M. Townsend, "Impact of Climate Change on Rice Production in Thailand," *American Economic Review* 99, no. 2 (May 2009): 1–10.

Our goal is to evaluate crop yield impacts from likely climate changes for Southeast Asia. To do so we link soil science crop modeling, weather simulators, and global climate change modeling into an integrated economic model of multistage rice production. The economic model is estimated with detailed monthly data on inputs, operations, and environmental data over a five year period. We then forecast impacts under two different future economic scenarios, one assuming high future global anthropogenic pollution emissions, and the other assuming low. We compare results of the integrated economic model with those of a biophysical model, inputting into both the stochastic realizations of a weather generator, calibrated against the present no-climate benchmark and against the two climate change scenarios—mild and severe. The more realistic forecasts from the socioeconomic model thus include important farmer behavioral/mitigation strategies. We discuss both aggregate/average impacts and heterogeneity.

Michael W. Binford, Tae Jeong Lee, and Robert M. Townsend, "Sampling Design for an Integrated Socioeconomic and Ecological Survey by Using Satellite Remote Sensing and Ordination," *Proceedings of the National Academy of Sciences* 101, no. 31 (August 2004): 11517–11522.

Environmental variability is an important risk factor in rural agricultural communities. Testing models requires empirical sampling that generates data that are representative in both economic and ecological domains. Detrended correspondence analysis of satellite remote sensing data were used to design an effective low-cost sampling protocol for a field study to create an integrated socioeconomic and ecological database when no prior information on ecology of the survey area existed. We stratified the sample for the selection of *tambons* from various preselected provinces in Thailand based on factor analysis of spectral land-cover classes derived from satellite data. We conducted the survey for the sampled villages in the chosen tambons. The resulting data capture interesting variations in soil productivity and in the timing of good and bad years, which a purely random sample would likely have missed. Thus, this database will allow tests of hypotheses concerning the effect of credit on productivity, the sharing of idiosyncratic risks, and the economic influence of environmental variability.

Policy Evaluation

Robert M. Townsend, *Financial Systems in Developing Economies: Growth, Inequality, and Policy Evaluation in Thailand* (New York: Oxford University Press), 2011.

Unique in its approach and in the variety of methods and data employed, this book is the first of its kind to provide an in-depth evaluation of the financial system of Thailand, a proto-typical Asian developing economy. Using a wealth of primary source qualitative and quantitative data, including survey data collected by the author, it evaluates the impact of specific financial institutions, markets for credit and insurance, and government policies on growth, inequality, and poverty at the macro, regional, and village level in Thailand. Useful not only as a guide to the Thai economy but more importantly as a means of assessing the impact that financial institutions and policy variation can have at the macro- and micro-level, including the distribution of gains and losses, this book will be invaluable to academics and policymakers with an interest in development finance.

Robert M. Townsend and Kenichi Ueda, "Welfare Gains from Financial Liberalization," *International Economic Review* 51, no. 3 (August 2010): 553–597.

Financial liberalization has been a controversial issue, as empirical evidence for growth enhancing effects is mixed. Here, we find sizable welfare gains from liberalization (cost to repression), though the gain in economic growth is ambiguous. We take the view that financial liberalization is a government policy that alters the path of financial deepening, while financial deepening is endogenously chosen by agents given a policy and occurs in transition toward a distant steady state. This history-dependent view necessitates the use of simulation analysis based on a growth model. Our application is a specific episode: Thailand from 1976 to 1996.

Robert M. Townsend, "Financial Markets and Poverty: An Algorithm for Policy-based Research and Research-based Policy" (chapter 1 in proceedings of 2004 Inter-American Development Bank conference).

This chapter explores the relationship between poverty and financial markets. The document serves as a guide for operations and policy on the one hand and for research on the other. But the chapter does not distinguish between these two uses. Rather, both are merged into a common goal: policy is based on research and research is geared toward generating policy conclusions. The starting point of each section of this chapter is an explicit structural model. A list of data that would be needed to test the model comes next, followed by an outline of exactly how the data would be used: that is, what procedures or tests would be employed in the analysis. The findings of the empirical work from the analysis are then presented. Then and only then are explicit, detailed recommendations for policy offered. The final section offers a few caveats, notes some weakness, and gives some directions for further efforts along this line.

Xavier Giné and Robert M. Townsend, "Evaluation of Financial Liberalization: A General Equilibrium Model with Constrained Occupation Choice," *Journal of Development Economics* 74, no. 2 (August 2004): 269–304.

The objective of this paper is to assess both the aggregate growth effects and the distributional consequences of financial liberalization as observed in Thailand from 1976 to 1996. A general equilibrium occupational choice model with two sectors, one without intermediation and the other with borrowing and lending is taken to Thai data. Key parameters of the production technology and the distribution of entrepreneurial talent are estimated by maximizing the likelihood of transition into business given initial wealth as observed in two distinct datasets. Other parameters of the model are calibrated to try to match the two decades of growth as well as observed changes in inequality, labor share, savings and the number of entrepreneurs. Without an expansion in the size of the intermediated sector, Thailand would have evolved very differently, namely, with a drastically lower growth rate, high residual subsistence sector, non-increasing wages but lower inequality. The financial liberalization brings welfare gains and losses to different subsets of the population. Primary winners are talented would-be entrepreneurs who lack credit and cannot otherwise go into business (or invest little capital). Mean gains for these winners range from 17 to 34 percent of observed, overall average household income. But liberalization also induces greater demand by entrepreneurs for workers resulting in increases in the wage and lower profits of relatively rich entrepreneurs, of the same order of magnitude as the observed overall average income of firm owners. Foreign capital has no significant impact on growth or the distribution of observed income.

Suchanan Tambunlertchai, "The Government's Helping Hand: A Study of Thailand's Agricultural Debt Moratorium" (PhD diss., University of Chicago, 2004).

This paper relates the empirical study on the effectiveness of Thailand's Agricultural Debt Moratorium Program (DMP). Under the DMP, small-scale farmers could reschedule their principle and interest repayments, or enter into a reduced-interest repayment scheme for a period of three years. The program came about as part of the government's effort to provide relief to farmers in times of economic tensions. The objective of the program, as put forth by the government, is to alleviate poverty among the agricultural households and use the period of relief to encourage structural changes in framers' operations. Implemented in April 2001, the DMP is set to end in September 2004. This study therefore aims to evaluate the impact of the DMP on its participants as the program approaches its end. The analyses focus on the changes in consumption, asset accumulation, and savings of the participating households. The study uses panel data collected from 2001, when the DMP was just being implemented, and from 2003, when the program had completed two-thirds of its lifetime. Findings indicate that the DMP has fallen short of its objectives, and, after two years, has not had significant impact on its participants. Furthermore, conditions imposed by the program on its participants may have been detrimental to its own objectives.

Inequality and National and Household Growth

Anan Pawasutipaisit and Robert M. Townsend, "Wealth Accumulation and Factors Accounting for Success" *Journal of Econometrics* 161, no. 1 (March 2011): 56–81.

We use detailed income, balance sheet, and cash flow statements constructed for households in a long monthly panel in an emerging market economy, and some recent contributions in economic theory, to document and better understand the factors underlying success in achieving upward mobility in the distribution of net worth. Wealth inequality is decreasing over time, and many households work their way out of poverty and lower wealth over the seven-year period. The accounts establish that, mechanically, this is largely due to savings rather than incoming gifts and remittances. In turn, the growth of net worth can be decomposed household by household into the savings rate and how productively that savings is used, the return on assets (ROA). The latter plays the larger role. ROA is, in turn, positively correlated with higher education of household members, younger age of the head, and with a higher debt/asset ratio and lower initial wealth, so it seems from cross-sections that the financial system is imperfectly channeling resources to productive and poor households. Household fixed effects account for the larger part of ROA, and this success is largely persistent, undercutting the story that successful entrepreneurs are those that simply get lucky. Persistence does vary across households, and in at least one province with much change and increasing opportunities, ROA changes as households move over time to higher-return occupations. But for those households with high and persistent ROA, the savings rate is higher, consistent with some micro founded macro models with imperfect credit markets. Indeed, high ROA households save by investing in their own enterprises and adopt consistent financial strategies for smoothing fluctuations. More generally, growth of wealth savings levels and/or rates are correlated with TFP and the household fixed effects that are the larger part of ROA.

Hyeok Jeong and Robert M. Townsend, "Growth and Inequality: Model Evaluation Based on an Estimation-Calibration Strategy," *Macroeconomic Dynamics Special Issue on Inequality* 12, no. S2 (September 2008): 231–84.

This paper evaluates two well-known models of growth with inequality that have explicit micro underpinnings related to household choice. With incomplete markets or transactions costs, wealth can constrain investment in business and the choice of occupation and also constrain the timing of entry into the formal financial sector. Using the Thai Socioeconomic Survey (SES), we estimate the distribution of wealth and the key parameters that best fit cross-sectional data on household choices and wealth. We then simulate the model economies for two decades at the estimated initial wealth distribution and analyze whether the model economies at those micro-fit parameter estimates can explain the observed macro and sectoral aspects of income growth and inequality change. Both models capture important features of Thai reality. Anomalies and comparisons across the two distinct models yield specific suggestions for improved research on the micro foundations of growth and inequality.

Hyeok Jeong and Robert M. Townsend, "Sources of TFP Growth: Occupational Choice and Financial Deepening," *Economic Theory Special Edition Honoring Edward Prescott* 32, no. 1 (July 2007): 179–221.

This paper explains and measures the sources of TFP by developing a method of growth accounting based on an integrated use of transitional growth models and micro data. We decompose total factor productivity (TFP) growth into the occupational-shift effect, financial-deepening effect, capital-heterogeneity effect, and sectoral-Solow-residuals. Applying this method to Thailand, which experienced rapid growth with enormous structural changes between 1976 and 1996, we find that 73 percent of TFP growth is explained by occupational shifts and financial deepening, without presuming exogenous technical progress. Expansion of credit is a major part. We also show the role of endogenous interaction between factor price dynamics and the wealth distribution for TFP.

Robert M. Townsend and Kenichi Ueda, "Financial Deepening, Inequality, and Growth: A Model-Based Quantitative Evaluation," *Review of Economic Studies* 73, no. 1 (January 2006): 251–293.

We propose a coherent, unified approach to the study of the linkages among economic growth, financial structure, and inequality, bringing together disparate theoretical and empirical literature. That is, we show how to conduct model-based quantitative research on transitional paths. With analytical and numerical methods, we calibrate and make tractable a prototype canonical model and take it to an application, namely, Thailand 1976 to 1996, an emerging market economy in a phase of economic expansion with uneven financial deepening and increasing inequality. We look at the expected path generated by the model and conduct robustness experiments. Because the actual path of the Thai economy is imagined here to be just one realization of many possible histories of the model economy, we construct a covariance-normalized squared error metric of closeness and find the best-fit simulation. We also construct a confidence region from a set of simulations and formally test the model. We broadly replicate the actual data and identify anomalies.

Liu Yang, "Unequal Provinces But Equal Families? An Analysis of Inequality and Migration in Thailand," in "Thailand in Essays on the Determinants and Consequences of Internal Migration" (PhD diss., University of Chicago, 2004).

In Thailand, gross provincial product is highly unequal while household income exhibits moderate between-province inequality. This paper introduces a dynamic model to analyze the link between migration and cross-province inequality. The wage differential drives rural-to-urban migration and in turn the wage rate at the destination is affected by total amount of migrant labor supply. Migration generates a net income gain for migrants, and they share that income gain with household members, remitting cash and goods. Remittances thus help redistribute income toward poor provinces, resulting in a lower level of cross-province inequality in household incomes. Simulations of migration, wages, inequality in production and inequality in income suggest that the benchmark model provides a good approximation to Thai reality. Fixed effects estimation shows a statistically significant effect of migration on income inequality: increasing the mean fraction of out-migrants to Bangkok by 1 percent leads to a 0.058 reduction in the average ratio of Bangkok's income to all other provinces (an elasticity of −0.11).

Hyeok Jeong, "Sources of Kuznets Dynamics in Thailand" (PhD diss., University of Chicago, 2000).

The Kuznets curve postulates a dynamic relationship between growth and income inequality for a given economy. These two aggregate phenomena are linked through compositional changes in individual characteristics when self-selection is constrained by personal wealth. This paper attempts to identify the crucial characteristics associated with this dynamic relationship, by studying the evolution of the income distribution in Thailand between 1976 and 1996, during which the economy experienced strong growth with diminution of poverty, but with a rapid increase in income inequality. Applying comprehensive decomposition analyses to the data from the Thai Socioeconomic Survey, this paper shows that growth and income distribution dynamics were closely related to an expansion of education and credit, and to an occupational transformation. These three factors account for 39 percent of the average income growth, 39 to 54 percent of poverty reduction depending on the poverty index, and 53 percent of increase in inequality. Each of these factors contributed to growth by a similar magnitude. However, the expansion of education and credit was concentrated among wealthy households and increased inequality while the transformation of occupation occurred mainly among middle class and reduced poverty.

Entrepreneurship and Financial Constraints

Alexander Karaivanov and Robert M. Townsend, "Dynamic Financial Constraints: Distinguishing Mechanism Design from Exogenously Incomplete Regimes" (working paper, 2012).

We formulate and solve a range of dynamic models of constrained credit/insurance that allow for moral hazard and limited commitment (and in some runs include hidden output and unobserved capital and investment). We compare them to full insurance and exogenously incomplete financial regimes (autarky, saving only, and borrowing and lending in a single asset). We develop computational methods based on mechanism design, linear programming, and maximum likelihood to estimate, compare, and statistically test these alternative dynamic models with financial/information constraints. Our methods can use both cross-sectional and panel data and allow for measurement error and unobserved heterogeneity. We estimate the models using data on Thai households running small businesses in two separate samples. We find that for the rural sample, the saving only and borrowing regimes provide the best fit using data on consumption, business assets, investment, and income from rural Thailand. Family and other networks are helpful in consumption smoothing there, as in a moral hazard constrained regime. In contrast, in urban areas, we find financial/information regimes that are decidedly less constrained, with the moral hazard model fitting best combined business and consumption data and with consumption and income data. We run numerous robustness checks in the Thai data and in Monte Carlo simulations and compare our maximum likelihood criterion with results from other metrics and data not used in the estimation.

Alexander Karaivanov, Anna L. Paulson, and Robert M. Townsend, "Distinguishing Limited Liability from Moral Hazard in a Model of Entrepreneurship," *Journal of Political Economy* 114, no. 1 (February 2006): 100–144.

We present and estimate a model in which the choice between entrepreneurship and wage work may be influenced by financial market imperfections. The model allows for limited liability, moral hazard, and a combination of both constraints. The paper uses structural techniques to estimate the model and identify the source of financial market imperfections using data from rural and semi-urban households in Thailand. Structural, nonparametric, and reduced-form estimates provide independent evidence that the dominant source of credit market imperfections is moral hazard. We reject the hypothesis that limited liability alone can explain the data.

Anna L. Paulson and Robert M. Townsend, "Financial constraints and entrepreneurship: Evidence from the Thai financial crisis," *Economic Perspectives* Federal Reserve Bank of Chicago 29, Third Quarter (2005): 34–48.

In this article, we provide some insights into how rural and semi-urban households in Thailand coped with the financial crisis. The results of this article also underscore the importance of carefully controlling for changes in the returns to non-entrepreneurial activity more generally. These findings help us to understand, for example, increases in self-employment observed in the U.S. during the recession that ended in November 2001. This article is organized as follows. First, we discuss some of the relevant related literature. Then, we provide more background on the impact of the Thai financial crisis, detail the financial environment in the survey areas, and describe the longitudinal data that we analyze. Next, we use regression analysis to examine the role of financial constraints in explaining patterns of entrepreneurship before, during, and after the crisis. Finally, we consider how to interpret these findings in the light of other trends in entrepreneurial characteristics over the period from 1997 to 2001.

Anna L. Paulson and Robert M. Townsend, "Entrepreneurship and Financial Constraints in Thailand," *Journal of Corporate Finance* 10, no. 2 (March 2004): 229–262.

We use new data from rural and semi-urban Thailand to examine how financial constraints affect entrepreneurial activity. The analysis uses nonparametric and reduced form techniques. The results indicate that financial constraints play an important role in shaping the patterns of entrepreneurship in Thailand. In particular, wealthier households are more likely to start businesses. Wealthier households are also more likely to invest more in their businesses and face fewer constraints. We also provide evidence that financial constraints place greater restrictions on entrepreneurial activity in the poor northeast compared to the more developed central region.

Alexander Karaivanov, "Financial Contracts and Occupational Choice" (PhD diss., University of Chicago, 2003).

Financial constraints and entrepreneurship are among the key factors affecting economic performance in developing countries. Emphasizing the link between the theory microfoundations and the data, the paper considers a heterogeneous agents' model of occupational choice with moral hazard under three financial contract regimes differing in their degree of market incompleteness: savings only, borrowing and lending, and insurance.

Using maximum likelihood estimation and statistical model comparison methods, I find evidence that the more advanced financial contract regimes allowing for borrowing or insurance provide a better fit with cross-sectional and time-series data from Thailand compared to the savings only regime. However, a direct comparison between the borrowing and lending and insurance regimes shows that neither of them can be rejected in favor of the other relative to the data. Augmenting the contracts with wealth-pooling lottery redistribution arrangements improves further the explanatory power of the model. A new numerical solution technique for incentive-constrained occupational choice models based on non-linear optimization is also proposed.

Risk and Insurance

Cynthia Kinnan and Robert M. Townsend, "Kinship and Financial Networks, Formal Financial Access and Risk Reduction," *American Economic Review* 102, no. 3 (May 2012): 289–293.

The importance of kinship networks in facilitating consumption smoothing and investment financing has been documented in many settings, but the channels through which networks matter are not well understood. We use detailed panel data on Thai households to study the financing devices used for consumption and investment by households with and without kin in the village, and with or without connections to financial institutions. Households that are connected to commercial and government banks directly or indirectly, through borrowing from connected households, achieve significantly better smoothing of consumption than unconnected households, controlling for the presence of kin and the effect of net worth. Investment, on the other hand, appears to be financed through kinship networks and through government banks: households with kin in the village and with connections to government banks display reduced sensitivity of investment to income, while connections to commercial banks do not significantly reduce investment sensitivity. We test the hypothesis that kin networks facilitate large investment expenditures through the relaxation of collateral constraints. The investment-smoothing benefit of kin networks is concentrated among households in occupations where the average investment size is high relative to net worth, suggesting that kin may act as implicit collateral permitting borrowing that cannot be collateralized with tangible assets.

Mauro Alem and Robert M. Townsend, "An Evaluation of Financial Institutions: Impact on Consumption and Investment Using Panel Data and the Theory of Risk-Bearing" (working paper, 2012).

The theory of the optimal allocation of risk and the Townsend Thai Data on financial transactions are used to assess the impact of the major formal and informal financial institutions of an emerging market economy. We link financial institution assessment to the actual impact on clients, rather than ratios and non-performing loans. We derive both consumption and investment equations from a common core theory with both risk and productive activities. The empirical specification follows closely from this theory and allows both OLS and IV estimation. We thus quantify the consumption and investment smoothing impact of financial institutions on households including those running farms and small businesses. A government development bank (BAAC) is shown to be particularly helpful in smoothing consumption and investment, in no small part through credit, consistent with its own operating system, which embeds an implicit insurance operation. Commercial banks are smoothing investment, largely through formal savings accounts. Other institutions seem ineffective by these metrics.

Pierre-André Chiappori, Krislert Samphantharak, Sam Schulhofer-Wohl, and Robert M. Townsend, "Heterogeneity and Risk-Sharing in Thai Villages" (working paper, 2011).

We measure heterogeneity in risk aversion among households in Thai villages using a full risk-sharing model and complement the results with a measure based on optimal portfolio choice. Among households with relatives living in the same village, full insurance cannot be rejected, suggesting that relatives provide something close to a complete-markets consumption allocation. There is substantial heterogeneity in risk preferences estimated from the full-insurance model, positively correlated in most villages with portfolio-choice estimates. The heterogeneity matters for policy: Although the average household would benefit from eliminating village-level risk, less-risk-averse households who are paid to absorb that risk would be worse off.

Cynthia Kinnan, "Distinguishing Barriers to Insurance in Thai Villages" (PhD diss., Massachusetts Institute of Technology, 2010).

A large body of evidence shows that informal insurance is an important risk-smoothing mechanism in developing countries but that this risk sharing is incomplete. Models of limited commitment, moral hazard, and hidden income have been proposed to explain the incomplete nature of informal insurance. Using the first-order conditions characterizing optimal insurance subject to each type of constraint, I show that the way history matters in forecasting consumption can be used to distinguish hidden income from limited commitment and moral hazard. This implication does not rely on a particular specification of the production technology or utility function. In a seven-year panel from rural Thailand, I show that neither limited commitment nor moral hazard can fully explain the relationship between income and consumption. In contrast, the predictions of the hidden income model are supported by the data.

Krislert Samphantharak and Robert M. Townsend, "Risk and Return in Village Economies" (working paper, 2010).

We present a model for the study of risk and return of household assets in village economies. The model yields similar insights and predictions to those derived from the traditional Capital Asset Pricing Model (CAPM) and the Consumption based Asset Pricing Model (CCAPM) in finance literature. We apply our model to the monthly panel data from a household survey in rural Thailand. First, we find that higher exposure to aggregate, non-diversifiable risks, as measured by household beta, or the co-movement of individual returns with the aggregate, is related to higher expected return on household assets. This finding is consistent with a major prediction from our model. The result is robust when we extend our definition of the aggregate economy or the market from village to province, and to the entire sample, or focus our definition to kinship networks within a village. The result is also robust when we control for household demography, asset sizes, and household occupations. We then use the prediction from the model to compute the risk-adjusted return for each household, i.e., the household alpha in CAPM terminology. Finally, we apply our model to the study of the village equity premium and estimate the implied coefficient of relative risk aversion. In contrast to "the equity premium puzzle" in the finance literature, our data at the less aggregate levels deliver estimates with a reasonably low magnitude. We also find that the larger the definition of the market, the more unreasonable magnitude of the implied risk aversion coefficient.

Pierre-André Chiappori, Hiroyuki Yamada, and Robert M. Townsend. "Sharing Wage Risk" (working paper, 2008).

Our paper introduces three innovations with respect to the standard literature. First, labor supply is explicitly recognized and modeled as an endogenous variable that responds to exogenous shocks. Actually, one of the main topics of the paper is precisely to investigate how adverse income shocks trigger changes in labor supply at the household, and possibly at the village level. Second, we consider variations in non-labor income, but also in wage. While price uncertainty arguably plays an important role in real life (if only because wage variations are a crucial component of income shocks), not much is known about optimal risk sharing in this context. In the paper, we provide an exhaustive, theoretical characterization of efficient risk sharing contracts in a general context of uncertainty on wages and incomes; as well as an empirical implementation. Finally, our setting is fairly general; in particular, it allows for different levels of risk aversion, both within and between households. We offer a detailed discussion of identification issues in this framework; we show, in particular, that preferences and the decision process are non-parametrically identifiable, and we show how long panels can be used in practice to achieve identification.

Robert M. Townsend and James Vickery, "Commodity Price Shocks, Consumption and Risk Sharing in Rural Thailand" (working paper, Essays in Banking and Risk Management, 2004).

International development organizations (including the World Bank and the International Taskforce on Commodity Risk Management) have begun to develop and implement strategies providing commodity price and weather insurance to primary producers in developing countries. But at present, we only have a limited understanding of how effective these nascent initiatives might be, and how they are likely to interact with existing risk-bearing mechanisms. In this paper, we examine how shocks to the price of rubber, an important but volatile Thai export commodity, affect the income, consumption, and intra-household remittances of rural Thai households. In contrast to related work on rainfall shocks, we find preliminary evidence that rubber price shocks are not well insured or smoothed—remittances, borrowing and saving play only small roles in ameliorating the effect of these shocks on the consumption of affected households. We argue that differences in the relative persistence of the two types of shocks provide a plausible reason why our results diverge so sharply from previous research, drawing on the literature on buffer stock models of consumption behavior and risk sharing with limited commitment.

James Vickery, "Essays in Banking and Risk Management" (PhD diss., Massachusetts Institute of Technology, 2004).

This thesis consists of three essays at the intersection of banking, corporate finance and macroeconomics. Unifying the essays are two themes: firstly a focus on how firms (chapter 1 and chapter 2) and individuals (chapter 3) insure against, and react to, sources of macroeconomic risk; secondly the role of financial institutions in the transmission of macroeconomic shocks.

Turning to specifics, chapter 1 is a theoretical and empirical examination of risk management behavior among small and medium sized firms, in particular firms' choices between fixed and adjustable rate loan contracts. (Although theory suggests small, privately held firms should have strong incentives to engage in risk management, such firms are rarely studied in empirical work.) I develop a simple agency model of risk management behavior, and then present several pieces of empirical evidence that suggest small US firms do use the banking system to help manage interest rate risk, based on microeconomic data on bank dependent US firms.

Chapter 2 presents evidence that banking relationships are most valuable to firms during periods of tight credit, in the extreme during a 'credit crunch'. Relationships alleviate delegated monitoring costs; when banks are credit constrained, these costs are extreme, so the informational advantage of relationships is magnified. I develop these intuitions using a simple agency model. Empirical evidence, based on data from a survey of manufacturing firms during the Asian financial crisis, supports the thesis. Several pieces of evidence also suggest my empirical results are not driven by the endogenous nature of bank relationship formation.

Financial institutions in co-operation with the World Bank and the International Taskforce on Commodity Risk Management have begun implementing strategies to provide commodity price and weather insurance in the developing world. In chapter 3 (joint with Professor Robert Townsend from the University of Chicago), we examine how shocks to the price of rubber, an important but volatile Thai export commodity, affect the income, consumption and intrahousehold remittances of rural Thai households. In contrast to related work on rainfall shocks, we find rubber price innovations are not well insured or smoothed—remittances, borrowing and saving play only small roles in ameliorating the effect of these shocks on the consumption of affected households. We argue that differences in the relative persistence of the two types of shocks provide a plausible reason for these divergent findings, drawing on the literature on buffer stock models of consumption behavior and risk sharing with limited commitment.

Robert M. Townsend and Jacob Yaron, "The Credit Risk Contingency System of an Asian Development Bank," *Economic Perspectives* 25, no. 3 (2001): 31–48.

Against the backdrop of the Asian financial crisis, we offer an analysis of one financial institution, a government-operated bank in Thailand, the Bank for Agriculture and Agricultural Cooperatives (BAAC). First, we provide a brief review of the theory being used in this evaluation of financial institutions and of empirical work in developing and developed economies using that theory. Then, we provide some background information on the BAAC, in the specific context of Thailand. Next, we describe the BAAC risk-contingency system, that is, its actual operating system and how it handles farmers experiencing adverse events. Then, we elaborate via a series of examples on appropriate ways to provision against possible nonpayment, given that underlying risk. We also tie provisioning and accounting standards to the optimal allocation of risk bearing in general equilibrium, inclusive of moral hazard problems. Next, with the costs of insurance well measured, we turn to a more detailed discussion of BAAC accounts and how they might be improved, so as to measure and evaluate better the portion of the Thai government subsidy that is effectively the payment of an insurance premium for farmers.

Robert M. Townsend, "Consumption Insurance: An Evaluation of Risk-Bearing Systems in Low-Income Economies." *Journal of Economic Perspectives* 9, no. 3 (Summer 1995): 83–102.

People face substantial, even catastrophic, risk throughout most of the developing countries of the world. The central nature of such risk raises three related issues. First, how covariate or insurable are these various risks? What markets or technologies are available to manage the risk? What financial institutions are available to offer implicit and explicit insurance? To answer these questions, this paper begins with a focus on income fluctuations and sources of data for three sample economies. The following section focuses on full insurance to get at the basic economics of risk bearing and insurance markets. This is followed with a section on empirical results and interpretation using consumption and income from the three economies. A following section addresses the important question of how consumption is actually smoothed within villages and regions. The last part of the paper focuses on incentive issues, looking at institutions in a manner informed by the mechanism design and contract theory literature.

Data Summaries

Esteban Puentes, "The Use of Financial Instruments in Thailand: 1997–2009" (2011).

Nathan Roth, "Data Summary for 1998–2007 Key Informant Resurvey: Growth, Inequality, and Organizational Design" (2010).

Adriana de la Huerta, "Data Summary for 1997 Household Survey" (2009).

Adriana de la Huerta, "Data Summary for 2005 Minister of Finance Initial Household Survey" (2009).

Akshay Birla, "BAAC Dataset Summary Document" (2009).

Liang Feng, "Data Summary for 1997 Key Informant Survey: Growth, Inequality, and Organizational Design" (2009).

Robert M. Townsend and Hiroyuki Yamada, "The Summary of the Monthly Household Survey of Thailand on Labor Issues" (2007).

Joseph Kaboski and Robert M. Townsend, "Founding and Membership of Local Financial Institutions in Semi-Urban and Rural Thailand" (1999).

This report summarizes survey results relating to the founding and membership of local-level financial institutions in four *changwats* (subregions) of Thailand—the semi-urban *changwats* of Chachoengsao and Lop Buri in the central region and the more rural Sisaket and Buriram in the poorer northeast region. The data used for this purpose are from an institutional survey administered in May 1997 (before the financial crisis hit). The 161 institutions surveyed consisted of rice banks, production credit groups (PCGs) and other financial institutions in the villages (90.6 percent) and/or *tambons* (9.4 percent) of these areas. This report addresses only the section of that survey that pertains to savings services offered.

The aims of this report are to describe the policies and experiences of the institutions with respect to their founding and membership over time. Section I focuses on the founding, specifically who started the institutions, when and with what resources they were established, and what types of training were involved with the founding. Section II examines the policies and history of the institution concerning membership. Where applicable, we attempt to compare the results from this institutional survey with those of the household survey. Both surveys are components of a larger survey project entitled Growth, Inequality and Organizational Design in Thailand.

Joseph Kaboski and Robert M. Townsend, "Savings Services of Local Financial Institutions in Semi-Urban and Rural Thailand" (1999).

This report summarizes the savings services at local-level financial institutions in four *changwats* (subregions) of Thailand—the semi-urban *changwats* of Chachoengsao and Lop Buri in the central region and the more rural Sisaket and Buriram in the poorer northeast region. The data used for this purpose are the result of an institutional survey administered in May 1997 (before the financial crisis hit). The 161 institutions surveyed consisted of rice banks, production credit groups (PCGs) and other financial institutions in the villages and/or tambons of these areas. This report summarizes only the section of that survey that pertains to savings services offered.

The aims of this report are to examine the extent and characteristics of the various types of savings services offered to members or customers of these financial institutions. Section I describes the types of savings accounts offered and the institutions' policies regarding savings accounts. Section II focuses on the institutions' history with savings services (the number of savers, total amount of savings, and interest rates) and the reasons for changes over time. Where applicable, we attempt to compare the results from this institutional survey with those of the household survey. Both surveys are components of a larger survey project entitled Growth, Inequality and Organizational Design in Thailand.

Notes

Introduction

1. Numbers indicated include but do not surpass October 2011.

2. Robert M. Townsend, Anna Paulson, Tae Jeong Lee, and Michael Binford. *Townsend Thai Project Initial Household Survey, 1997* [Computer file]. (Chicago: Social Sciences Computing Services, the University of Chicago [Producer & distributor, 1st release] 2005). Questionnaires from the baseline study are posted online at http://cier.uchicago.edu/data/baseline-survey.shtml.

3. Robert M. Townsend, *The Medieval Village Economy* (Princeton, NJ: Princeton University Press, 1993).

4. Robert M. Townsend, "Risk and Insurance in Village India," *Econometrica* 62, no. 3 (May 1994), 539–591.

5. National Institute of Child Health and Human Development grant 5R01HD027638.

6. National Science Foundation grant 0649302.

Chapter 1

1. A conversion rate of 1 baht (THB) = 0.030 USD will be used here and throughout the remainder of the text.

2. Anne Johnson, ed., "Who Gets What and How: Challenges for the Future," *TDRI Quarterly Review* 9, no. 1 (March 1994), 3–7.

Chapter 2

1. Such traits represent Thai cultural values and were an asset in challenging situations.

Chapter 3

1. The monthly survey is discussed in chapter 4.

Chapter 4

1. None of the monthly survey villages overlapped with the annual resurvey.

Chapter 6

1. "Village Fund Research Result Exposed: Foreigner Proves that Debt Increases and Assets Decrease," *Matichon Daily*, August 17, 2004, http://www.nidambe11.net/ekonomiz/2004q3/article2004aug18p3.htm.

Chapter 8

1. The percentage of re-interviews is highest in provinces where agricultural production is prevalent, due to the diverse number of crops.

Epilogue

1. Pierre-André Chiappori, Krislert Samphantharak, Sam Schulhofer-Wohl, and Robert M. Townsend, "Heterogeneity and Risk-Sharing in Thai Villages" (working paper, 2011).

2. Chiappori, Samphantharak, Schulhofer-Wohl, and Townsend (2011).

3. Joseph Kaboski and Robert M. Townsend, "Policies and Impact: An Analysis of Village-Level Microfinance Institutions," *Journal of the European Economic Association* 3, no. 1 (March 2005), 1–50.

4. Abhijit Banerjee, Emily Breza, and Robert M. Townsend, "Productive Heterogeneity and Household Investment in Rural Thailand" (working paper, 2010).

5. Adriana de la Huerta, "Microfinance in Rural and Urban Thailand: Policies, Social Ties and Successful Performance" (PhD diss., University of Chicago, 2011).

6. Archawa Paweenawat and Robert M. Townsend, "Villages as Small Open Economies" (working paper, 2011).

7. John Felkner and Robert M. Townsend, "The Geographic Concentration of Enterprise in Developing Countries," *Quarterly Journal of Economics* 125, no. 4 (2011), 2005–2061.

8. Juliano Assuncao, Sergey Mityakov, and Robert M. Townsend, "Ownership Matters: The Geographical Dynamics of BAAC and Commercial Banks in Thailand" (working paper, 2012).

9. Mauro Alem and Robert M. Townsend, "An Evaluation of Financial Institutions: Impact on Consumption and Investment Using Panel Data and the Theory of Risk-Bearing" (working paper, 2012).

10. Cynthia Kinnan and Robert M. Townsend, "Kinship and Financial Networks, Formal Financial Access, and Risk Reduction," *American Economic Review* 103, no. 3 (2012), 289–293.

11. Alem and Townsend (2012).

12. Parit Sripakdeevong and Robert M. Townsend, "Refinancing Loans" (working paper, 2012).

13. Narapong Srivisal, "How Consumption, Capital Formation and Wealth in Rural Thai Villages Respond to Supply Shocks to Sources of Funds" (PhD diss., University of Chicago, 2012).

Index

Abhisit Vejjajiva, Prime Minister, 84
Adam, Aleena, 70–71
Agricultural cooperatives, 105
Agricultural production, 42–43, 60, 67–69, 74
Annual surveys, xi, xiv, xviii, xix, 27–38, 76. *See also* Urban annual surveys
attrition rates, xi, 90
baseline data, 90
and baseline survey, 33–34
data cleaning, 65
number of households/villages surveyed, xi, 29
planning for, 46
Risk and Response Module, 60
rural communities as focus of, 29, 46
validation process, 91
Applied general equilibrium analysis (AGE), 7. *See also* General equilibrium models
Asian financial crisis, 1997, 27–28
Ask-and-check control system, 32–33
Assets, return on. *See* Return on assets (ROA)

Baht, devaluation of, 27–28
Bank for Agricultural and Agricultural Cooperatives (BAAC), xviii, xix, 1, 2, 4, 7–8, 123
branch locations, 104
economic importance of, 106
informal access to, 105
Nakon Chaisi area farmers, loans to, 7
risk reduction, role in, 105
surveys, xi, 8, 9, 18, 29
Thai Project expansion funded by, 70–71, 75

Banks. *See* Financial institutions
Baseline survey, xi, xiv, 11–26, 61, 76
and annual surveys, 33–34
Buriram, 21–22
Chachoengsao Province, 25–26
follow-up interviews, 18–19
history of, xvii–xviii
Lop Buri Province, 23–25
and monthly surveys, 41
Benchmark standards, 99
Benefits, staff, 54–55
Big Survey. *See* Baseline survey
Binford, Michael, 9–10, 60
Borrowing. *See* Loans and credit
Buddhist monks, 57–59
Budget, TFRP, 53–55, 73, 85. *See also* Funding
Buriram Province, xi, xviii, 8, 37, 51–52, 76
baseline survey, 22
description of, 21
field office, 34
location of, 15–16
monthly surveys, 39, 44, 49, 50
urban annual surveys, 80
Business activity, 87, 99. *See also* Entrepreneurship; Microfinance
flow of funds, 106–107
return on assets, 102
and risk, 100
small businesses, effect on national economy of, 106
as survey component, 9, 10, 29, 39, 45, 80, 94
of TFRP staff, 90–91
in urban areas, 80–82

open economies, villages as, 103–104,
109
return on assets and intermediation, 102
risk, shocks, and insurance, 100–102
Village headmen. *See* Key informants
(village headmen)
Villages, xviii
annual surveys, number of villages
included in, 29
monthly surveys, number of villages
included in, 40–41

Water measurements, 8, 18, 41–43
Wealth, 36, 104. *See also* Entrepreneurship;
Poverty reduction
economic inequality, 11, 70, 114–118
and flow of funds, 107
income shocks, effect on vulnerability
to, 101–102
as survey component, 9, 31, 93–94
Wutthimethi, Yuwat, 4, 17

Yala Province, xi, xviii, 70, 73–76, 93
Yingluck Shinawatra, Prime Minister, 84